Her Place at the Table

"More than ever before, negotiation is a critical competency for success in business. *Her Place at the Table* offers valuable approaches for any woman hungry to make the most of her career potential."

—Barbara Desoer, president,
Consumer Products, Bank of America

"More women are stepping into senior leadership positions and facing the day-to-day challenges and resistance to their leadership. *Her Place at the Table* provides excellent advice to these new women leaders. Here is a guide to help all women executives maneuver the corporate landscape and avoid the pitfalls that could impact their success as leaders."

—Lynn Martin, former Secretary of Labor and chair of
Deloitte & Touche's Council on the Advancement
of Women; and Sue Molina, retired partner and former
national director of the Initiative for the Retention and
Advancement of Women, Deloitte & Touche

"New leadership assignments are fraught with challenges. In this engaging and useful book, the authors analyze the leadership experiences of over one hundred women and develop a plan for negotiating a 'place at the [leadership] table.' Anyone trying to navigate today's organizational landscape will learn from the insights in *Her Place at the Table*."

—Patricia O'Brien, deputy dean, Harvard College

"*Her Place at the Table* provides key practical advice for women leaders who must navigate the 'organizational minefields.' The questions alone are an essential part of any leader's toolkit!"

—Rayona Sharpnack, president,
Institute for Women's Leadership, Inc.

HER PLACE AT THE TABLE

A WOMAN'S GUIDE
TO NEGOTIATING FIVE KEY CHALLENGES
TO LEADERSHIP SUCCESS

Completely Updated

Deborah M. Kolb
Judith Williams
Carol Frohlinger

JOSSEY-BASS
A Wiley Imprint
www.josseybass.com

Published by Jossey-Bass
A Wiley Imprint
989 Market Street, San Francisco, CA 94103-1741—www.josseybass.com

Jossey-Bass books and products are available through most bookstores. To contact Jossey-Bass directly call our Customer Care Department within the U.S. at 800-956-7739, outside the U.S. at 317-572-3986, or fax 317-572-4002.

Jossey-Bass also publishes its books in a variety of electronic formats. Some content that appears in print may not be available in electronic books.

Library of Congress Cataloging-in-Publication Data

Kolb, Deborah M.
   Her place at the table : a woman's guide to negotiating five key challenges to leadership success / Deborah M. Kolb, Judith Williams, Carol Frohlinger.
      p. cm.
   Includes bibliographical references and index.
      ISBN 978-0-470-63375-5 (pbk); ISBN 978-0-470-94466-0 (ebk); ISBN 978-0-470-94467-7 (ebk); ISBN 978-0-470-94468-4 (ebk)
1. Women executives. 2. Leadership. 3. Leadership in women. 4. Management.
I. Williams, Judith, 1942- II. Frohlinger, Carol, 1953- III. Title
HD6054.3 .K65 2010
658.4'09208—dc22

2010023110

Printed in the United States of America
UPDATED EDITION
PB Printing   10 9 8 7 6 5

CONTENTS

APPENDIX B 206

What Organizations Can Learn from How Women
Leaders Negotiate the Five Challenges

TAKING YOUR PLACE AT THE LEADERSHIP TABLE

Questions Will Be Asked

We are experiencing a historic shift in the workplace. For the first time in U.S. history, women comprise the majority of the workforce. In medium-sized and large corporations women hold 50 percent of middle management jobs. The number of women who have started their own businesses has grown exponentially.[1] And more women than ever before are serving as their family's primary breadwinner.[2]

Yet leadership roles in major institutions still elude women. According to Catalyst, women hold less than 3 percent of the chief executive jobs in the Fortune 500 (and that is the highest number ever) and less than 16 percent of corporate officer jobs (a number that has remained static since 2002). Another recent Catalyst study of the top two thousand global companies indicated only twenty-nine CEOs were women.[3] It was not supposed to be this way.

During the past decade, we heard so much about new models of leadership—post-heroic and servant leadership styles were heralded as the new paradigm. Organizations were supposedly abandoning archaic command-and-control hierarchies in favor of flatter, more collaborative organizational structures. These new and enlightened organizations would favor teamwork and cooperation over superstars and competition. Management consultants, researchers, and academics predicted this shift would be a boon for women.[4] In the post-heroic era, the "female advantage" in leadership seemed admirably suited to meet the global challenges of the new economy.[5]

Indeed, a series of research studies give credence to this theory. The "female advantage" produces better results. Companies with higher percentages of women directors and senior managers deliver better returns to shareholders and outperform competitors.[6] Why? Well, for starters, companies with higher percentages of women at the top are choosing the best leaders from a broader, more diverse talent pool than other companies. A gender-diverse leadership team is better equipped to relate to its customer base. (Eighty-five percent of all consumer purchasing decisions are made by women.[7]) And then there is the theory that women are more likely to lead in a participative manner that promotes teamwork—and teamwork leads to better firm performance.[8]

It is obvious that it is more than just the proportion of women in leadership that accounts for these results. Certain firms have organizational cultures and work practices that make it possible for women to move into leadership roles and these women in turn contribute to their organization's success.

Given these impressive results, why are women still finding it so difficult to get to the top of an organization?

IT'S NOT BECAUSE WOMEN LACK TALENT

Much research has been done to assess the performance of women in the workplace. The data reveals both bosses and subordinates rate women highly on leadership skills, including goal setting and aggressively pursuing those goals.[9] And women hold their own when compared with men, not only on the attributes we associate with women—teamwork, rewarding, and giving feedback, but also on such critical characteristics as emotional intelligence, outside orientation, designing and aligning structures, and tenacity. The theory that women are risk-averse has been debunked.[10] Finally, a new report finds the general public believes women have what it takes to be leaders in today's world. The only trait on which men were rated higher than women was decisiveness.[11]

And yet the same research that shows the strengths of women at work also supports the adage that women are judged on their performance while men are judged on their potential. Despite strong showing on leadership skills, it is men, rather than women, who are more likely to be seen as strong leaders.

IT'S NOT BECAUSE THERE AREN'T ENOUGH WOMEN IN THE PIPELINE

The pipeline—the number of available women in the pool of those "promotable"—is often singled out by corporate executives as a key reason why more women don't hold leadership positions. However, statistics suggest the pipeline is well supplied with women in business and the professions. Women constitute 39.4 percent of MBA graduates in 2009, up from 34 percent in 2005.[12] And women have graduated from law school for the past twenty years at roughly the same rate as men—yet they remain very poorly represented in law firm leadership.[13]

IT'S NOT BECAUSE WOMEN AREN'T INTERESTED

More recently, it has become common to look to women, and the choices they make, to explain their meager representation in leadership. That women voluntarily withdraw from the workplace—the so-called opt-out revolution—to have families and seek more balance in their lives—has become a common refrain among corporate leadership and the mainstream media.[14] In reality, between 1984 and 2004 the number of college-educated women with children who opted out of careers did not change very much at all   the number of women working outside the home remained stable at 70 percent.[15] In fact, when women do leave the workplace—when the pipeline leaks—it is often because of organizational issues—lack of challenge, inflexible work arrangements, and blocked careers—not because they opt out for family.[16]

IT'S NOT BECAUSE WOMEN DON'T ASK

Just as the women who leave corporations are blamed for the poor representation of women at the top, so are the women who stay. "They don't ask" is the other common excuse for why women don't get promoted.[17] If they don't have the requisite line experience it is because they have not stepped up and asked for it. If they have gotten stuck in undesirable corporate backwaters, it is because they didn't negotiate for something else. Yet we know that women do ask when issues matter to them—and when they can connect what is good for them to what is good for their organizations.[18]

So if women do have the talent, do remain in the game, and are interested in moving up, then what is the problem?

It's complicated. From what we know about organizations and how they function, it turns out women face a number of challenges that require them to negotiate a host of issues that their male colleagues rarely face. We, and others, call them "second-generation" gender issues.[19]

While first-generation issues involve clear-cut acts of bias, blatant discrimination, and perhaps harassment—the stuff of class action lawsuits—second-generation issues are more subtle—and in many ways more difficult to address because they are an inherent part of an organization's culture and work practices. These practices may look gender neutral—"we promote based solely on merit" or "our best employees are willing to do what it takes, 24/7"—but in fact they are likely to have differential impacts on men and women.

Professing to promote based "on merit" overlooks the intrinsic biases that often favor male leadership qualities. This practice also dismisses just how critical it is for leadership candidates to have networks that include the right people to act as sponsors.[20] These sponsorships tend to fall along gender lines, meaning there are more men sponsoring men, and this is true for both men of color and white men.[21] And being available 24/7 has a differential impact on people who have outside commitments.[22] The reality is women still shoulder much of the household responsibilities.[23] Research by Shelley Correll and her colleagues show mothers pay a penalty. Even with comparable credentials and experience, mothers were seen as less competent and promotable.[24]

These biases are deep-seated and rooted in firmly held beliefs. Even when a woman does not serve as a primary caregiver, her employer might make that assumption. For a woman to establish herself at the leadership table, she must answer questions that often are not even asked out loud.

Of course, all new leaders are tested and face challenges to some degree. People do not automatically throw their support to a new leader; they are more likely to adopt a wait-and-see attitude, but women leaders may face hyper scrutiny.[25] And this hyper scrutiny can be traced to some of the second-generation gender issues women face.

We have identified four questions that will almost certainly surround the appointment of a woman to a leadership role. Before she can get on with the business of leading, she has to address and deal with them. This can be tricky because often the women and her employer aren't even aware that some or all of these questions are in play.

- Is she a good fit for the role?
- Can she be both a woman and a leader?
- Has she demonstrated leadership capability?
- Will her personal life get in the way?

Is She a Good Fit for the Role?

Some jobs or roles are seen to fit one sex or the other. For example, helping professions like nursing and social work are often seen as feminine because they fit society's ideas of female nurturing, whereas firefighting and truck driving are labeled masculine because they emphasize brawn.[26] Many roles are conceived as masculine and then come to be seen as more suitable and attractive for men, reinforcing the perception that only men are suited for them.[27] Leadership has been labeled one of those roles.[28] Because leadership is perceived to reflect more masculine values, women are less likely to be seen as having leadership potential—not everyone has read the studies we cited earlier!

In one financial services firm, for example, promotion of partners into leadership roles was based on selling skills—*rainmaking*—something male partners were more successful at than their female counterparts.[29] Whether this was a result of different skill sets or merely differential access to client decision makers is not clear, but the outcome was that women were not put forth for leadership roles because leaders at this firm were the ones who developed business. To be considered for these top roles, women needed to negotiate for them. They had to reframe the decision-making process and even perhaps challenge the existing criteria for aspiring leaders—was selling really the most important leadership skill? What other skills would add value? How?

Firmly held assumptions that the work men have traditionally done is more important than so-called women's work position men as superior and more suited to leadership roles.[30] These beliefs can become self-fulfilling prophecies and can affect a woman's perception of herself. They can adversely impact how able she is to advocate for her own career. Not only must she convince herself that she can make the role into one that fits her skills and needs so she can succeed in it, she must also be prepared to make others comfortable with a reconfigured view of what that leadership role will look like.

This can also create challenges when she has to deal with opportunities she has not sought and does not particularly want. Aspiring leaders are expected to willingly take on developmental opportunities—to refuse may preclude other offers. This norm may work well for males, who are likely to be offered developmental opportunities in key strategic positions, but it does not necessarily work as effectively for women. The late Ellen Gabriel, who launched the Women's Initiative at Deloitte & Touche, observed that when the CEO approached her to take on the project, it was but just another example of a woman being offered a "human resource" assignment.[31] While male colleagues were challenged with strategic assignments that promised direct benefits to the bottom line, women were routinely asked to help with recruiting or to serve on diversity or performance management task forces. Women, after all, were good at these assignments. They are good at being strong number twos, chiefs of staff, where their contributions are likely to be invisible. They are, in one organization, asked to take on acting leadership roles. Once the women have succeeded in these roles, however, the positions somehow go to somebody else. Often women are asked to help out another leader who is having difficulty and so see their own work suffer.

There is another wrinkle to this. Generally, it is unwise politically to say no when presented with these so-called opportunities. Refusing to help clean up a department or assist a colleague can damage an aspiring leader's team-player status. As a result, under an unstated obligation to accept assignments, women can be channeled into roles that proffer fewer chances of enhancing their careers and do not answer the question of whether or not they are "leadership material." This is more than just a question of asking; it requires negotiating the fit—how a role will be defined and assessed, its duration as well as what follows from it—all topics we address in this book.

Can She Be Both a Woman and a Leader?

There is no better example of this question than what we witnessed during the 2008 presidential election. Hillary Clinton, in particular, was both chastised for being too masculine—"Hillary Clinton Is a Man and I Won't Vote for Him"—and then questioned about her toughness when she became emotional. Similarly, Margaret Thatcher was called "Attila the Hen"; Golda Meir, Israel's first female prime minister, was "the only man in the Cabinet"; and Angela Merkel, the current chancellor of Germany, has been dubbed "the iron frau."[32] Invoking these contradictory messages in the political arena reflects what researchers have found consistently when it comes to leadership.

The attributes we value in male leaders—being assertive, authoritative, and decisive—tend not be seen as either attractive or typical of women. We expect men to take charge and women to take care.[33] It is the classic double bind.

When women do assert themselves, they face a likeability versus competence challenge.[34] Frank Flynn and Cameron Mitchell conducted an experiment with their MBA students at Columbia University.[35] Using "Heidi Roizen," a Harvard Business School case about an entrepreneur, they gave one section of their students the "Heidi" case and the other students the "Howard Roizen" case. Howard's was the same case as Heidi's but with a different name. Students were asked to evaluate the style, likeability, and competence of both Howard and Heidi and to decide whether they would hire them. Both entrepreneurs were found equally competent and effective. Howard, however, was seen as more genuine and likable and more likely to be hired. Heidi, on the other hand, was seen as self-promoting, power hungry, and aggressive. A huge volume of other research reinforces these findings—when women are seen as competent leaders, they are not liked; when they are liked, they are not respected.[36] It is worth noting that the more women in leadership roles in an organization, the less pronounced this double bind becomes.[37]

All new leaders need to negotiate to create legitimacy in their role, but the question of femininity puts additional issues on the table for women leaders.[38] In this book, we help women answer it by connecting their interests to what is good for the organization. If a woman can clearly articulate that connection, she is more secure in asking for what she needs and others in the organization begin to get more comfortable with the idea that a "feminine" woman can indeed be a leader.[39]

Has She Demonstrated Leadership Capability?

All four of the questions about women leaders we discuss here are in some sense tests of legitimacy and credibility. But this question gets to the core of demonstrating whether or not women can truly have what it takes to be a leader. Establishing credibility as a leader can be an uphill campaign for women for a number of reasons.

As noted, study after study has shown that women are seen to have the strategic, organizational, and interpersonal skills that leaders need and are often rated higher on these skills than their male counterparts.[40] But Joyce Fletcher suggests there is a disconnect between the leadership skills women are seen to have and the credit they get for them.[41] That may be caused by the ways that women display these skills. Women tend to do so in a more relational way and so their skills are not credited as evidence of leadership competence but just "what women do."[42]

It also may be that a woman's leadership accomplishments are not as generally recognized because they take place under the radar, in the quiet accomplishment of an organization's goals. Joyce Fletcher calls this "invisible work."[43] In her study of engineers, she shows how some of the women engineers—the ones who try to anticipate problems before they happen, seek to integrate the work of others, and try to build a team—have their work disappear. While these actions could be seen as leading and signaling innovation, instead they may be discounted as women "just being nice" or wanting to be liked. Joanne Martin, in reflecting on her own experiences as a faculty member at Stanford Business School, also describes the invisible work women and minority faculty members perform—representing diversity viewpoints on a committee or task force, and advising and counseling graduate students and junior faculty. This work, while expected and definitely time-consuming—reducing time available for teaching and scholarship—doesn't count toward the all-important tenure and promotion decisions.[44]

A third explanation is that a woman's track record, like a man's, may be marred by some mistakes and failures. The difference, and therefore the problem, may be that a woman may have more of these mistakes than her male colleagues for two reasons. As we discuss in detail in Chapters One and Four, a woman may have been offered more turnaround challenges, which are inherently riskier. In their study of the "glass cliff," Ryan and Haslam show that when a firm's performance is on the decline, those in charge are more likely to appoint a woman to a board position or the C-suite.[45] And more often than not, women leaders are recruited from the outside, a position that makes it more difficult to deliver on performance.[46]

The glass cliff phenomenon can also be seen at levels below the most senior where women are tapped to make change. In one organization, for example, managers, especially women, were routinely asked to help fix situations where there were problems. Often this involved taking a job with a lesser title, say an "acting" role, for which they might not get credit, or being denied compensation for saving a major client. In one situation, a star female professional at a software solutions firm was asked to save a relationship with the firm's largest client. Three months and over a half million dollars of additional orders later, the relationship was secured, but the woman received no commission on the additional sales she had secured, nor did she receive a promotion. Instead, she went back to the job she'd been slated for before turning the client relationship around.[47]

While success may not be recognized and rewarded, failure is often quite visible. In yet another organization, mistakes tended to follow women more, in part because their male colleagues had strong networks and key sponsors high up in the organization who helped them recover—a situation that was less true for women.[48]

Finally, the evaluation of whether a woman has demonstrated leadership competence may reflect a more widely based phenomenon—an inherent bias against women and their credentials and performance. Virginia Valian summarizes the research that shows that in professional work settings men tend to be overrated and women underrated.[49] Résumé studies reveal that with the exact same experiences and skills, men are judged more favorably than women for both hiring and promotion.[50] Recent work suggests that organizations with strong merit-based systems are even more likely to reflect this bias.[51] When gender is rendered invisible, these biases disappear.

Claudia Goldin and Cecilia Rouse reviewed the results of auditions for symphony orchestras when the musician auditioned behind a screen so that their gender not revealed. Using the screen increased the probability that a woman would get a position in the orchestra by 250 percent![52] Because most of us will never have a screen masking our gender, in this book we show how women can claim value for their experiences and expertise and how they can enlist the support of others to overcome bias.

Will Her Personal Life Get in the Way?

In many cultures, up until quite recently, paid employment was seen as the domain of men while family responsibilities belonged to women. As women have joined the workforce in equal numbers, not surprisingly the issue of whether it is possible to hold leadership jobs and integrate them with a full family life has become a significant issue for women and the organizations that employ them. In 1990 Joan Acker coined the term "the ideal worker" to designate the person who is willing to put work before all else, whose time to spend at work is unlimited, and for whom the demands of family, community, and personal life are secondary or at least rendered invisible in the workplace.[53] Crisis-oriented work patterns, unbounded meeting times and places, and the need to put in face time impact who is seen as an ideal worker and who is not.[54] While this model—often called masculine—does not suit either men or women very well, it persists. Indeed, with the advent of extreme jobs and 24/7 expectations, the conflict between responsibilities for family and success at work have been exacerbated.[55]

Women, because they can become or are mothers, are particularly disadvantaged by the "ideal worker" paradigm. Motherhood is presumed to interfere with a women's commitment and willingness to put in the time and work necessary to accomplish the job even if there is no evidence for any particular woman to prove this so.[56] In one organization, for example, assignments to large, important clients were based on the belief that professionals would be able to stick with that client for the long haul. Concerns about *future* maternity and child care leaves had the effect of precluding women from consideration in these roles, which were critical to becoming leaders in the firm.[57] The assumption is typically made that, faced with the demands of her work and family, a woman will chose the latter. The reality, however, is that it is the inflexibility of the workplace , and unresponsive bosses, that causes some women to leave and others to tone down their ambitions.[58]

A woman will confront the "ideal worker" conundrum at many stages of her career, a fact that impacts the kinds of experiences she accrues on her route to leadership. Defined promotion schedules, such as tenure decisions in universities and admission to partnerships in financial service and law firms, create a well-articulated clash between a biological window for childbirth and child rearing with "up or out" career decisions.[59] Mothers are routinely offered less desirable assignments and lower compensation than women without children.[60] That makes high-achieving women less likely to make use of flexible work policies.[61] And *if they do take advantage of flex options,* they are often confronted with resistant bosses who, all things being equal, prefer the "ideal worker." Women push back on these assumptions by negotiating time commitments and flexibility, issues that matter to them.[62]

This book does not presume to provide a total solution to this question, for it really requires organizations to abandon the ideal worker hurdle for both women and men.[63] However, it does provide creative examples of how successful women have answered this question as they have taken on leadership roles.

ABOUT THIS BOOK

The idea for this book began germinating as we coached senior women to negotiate their places at the leadership table. Right from the start we were struck by the recurring questions they had to answer—first to secure leadership positions and then to establish their legitimacy in the role. It is critical for women to recognize these second-generation issues as they compete for and take on demanding and visible new assignments. If a woman ignores these questions, it can undercut her authority with others and undermine the self-confidence she needs to establish her place at the leadership table.

In this book we chart how women leaders—people who may not make the headlines but are making real differences in their organizations—understand and respond to these often unarticulated yet persistent questions. We interviewed more than a hundred women. The group was evenly divided between women embarking on their first leadership positions and those who were assuming assignments with increased responsibility. Our sample was by no means scientific, nor did it reflect the distribution of women within the leadership population generally. The majority of our sample held line positions or were moving into key staff jobs after significant experience on the line. They covered the spectrum of opportunities—small companies, large corporations, foundations. They came from the public and the private sectors. The highest concentration was in professional services (including banking, accounting, and law), health care, and technology, where software sales and marketing and biotechnology predominated.

What our interviews told us was that—contrary to laboratory research findings that women don't ask—the women portrayed in this book did ask. They knew what they needed to succeed and they negotiated for those things. They asked because these issues mattered to them.

These findings were reinforced in a complementary study. In that study, we surveyed more than five hundred women about their experiences negotiating for what they needed to be successful in a leadership role. More than 50 percent of this sample had a high proclivity to negotiate and those who did reported higher performance reviews and were more likely to be developed as leaders than those who did not. Interestingly, the negotiators were also more satisfied with their jobs and less likely to express an interest in leaving their organizations.[64] We found that what was critical for them in their negotiations was knowing exactly what to ask for.[65] Knowing what to ask enables a woman to confidently negotiate what she needs to succeed. We have organized these critical "asks" around five major challenges that require negotiation when a woman takes on any leadership role:

- Intelligence
- Backing of key players
- Resources
- Buy-in
- Making a difference

Intelligence: To successfully negotiate, one needs good information. That information runs the gamut from understanding what the requirements of a role are to knowing why you are the one tapped for it and identifying where the barriers to your success might lie. In the process of gathering this information, the women could test what kind of fit they would be for the role they were considering. Information also helped them figure out exactly what they needed to negotiate for, so that the role would be a good fit for them in both the near and longer term. Gathering intelligence also gave them helpful insights about the organization's culture so that they could anticipate the kinds of questions that might come up about their leadership competence and even about their personal commitments and then prepare to handle them.

Backing of key players: Legitimacy in a leadership role is not something that can be assumed. All leadership roles are in some sense a stretch—and additional questions will be asked about any woman who takes on such a role. That is why negotiating to have key sponsors support and then make the strategic case for their appointment is necessary but not sufficient. The women we interviewed understood that this kind of support is not a one-time thing but must be negotiated again and again over time as different challenges present themselves.

Resources: In the best of times, securing resources for innovation can be a challenge. In a constricted economy, it becomes a major hurdle. The important point about resources is not just that we need them to get things done but that they are important symbolically. Perceptions of the power and influence of a new leader is often judged by the leader's ability to secure resources. The women understood this and showed creativity in how they aligned their needs with those of strategic objectives of their organizations, built coalitions to partner in getting resources, and figured out ways to build support for their requests over time. Connecting what they needed to what was good for their organization was a guiding principle for all of the women. In doing this, they felt more confident asking for resources and were less likely to suffer backlash for asking.

Buy-in: Gaining support for an agenda is a negotiation that occurs at the individual, team, and systemic levels. A leader will most likely face resistance when trying to enact any change—big or small. Negotiating around this resistance involves understanding people's legitimate reasons for disagreeing and finding ways to address them through creative problem solving. Enlisting others in collaborative problem solving requires demonstrating the potential benefits of change and the costs associated with failing to get on board. In orchestrating buy-in, the leader needs to build a winning coalition of stakeholders and block opposing coalitions from forming. This is key for women if they are going to succeed in moving their agendas forward.

Making a difference: All the women we interviewed wanted to have a positive impact on their organizations. And indeed, many of them did. The challenge for women may not be making a difference. Instead, it may be getting credit for what they do. The invisible work of team building and integration can go unnoticed, but claiming value can unleash a challenge for women. Women who take credit invite backlash for being unfeminine and self-promoting. To claim their value, the women we interviewed focused on what needed to be done to meet the strategic and unmet needs of different groups in their organizations. When they claimed value, they did so in a currency that had value to others in the organization. Once the value they created was visible to others, it provided a platform to build on—within their own teams and across the organization.

In structuring this book, we have devoted a chapter to each of the five challenges. After exploring some of the traps that can undermine a leader's efforts, we lay out a set of strategic moves that document the ways in which the women we interviewed negotiated around these challenges. We focus on the stories they told of what they did and how they did it. In this way, the book provides a clear road map for what a woman leader needs to negotiate for if she wants to succeed. Each chapter is anchored by an ongoing case that shows the ways in which strategic moves can be mobilized over time and in concert with one another. Finally, we provide a guide to help you get ready to negotiate your own situation at work.*

Her Place at the Table builds upon the principles of the "shadow negotiation" that we describe in *Everyday Negotiation: Managing the Hidden Agendas of Bargaining*. As people bargain over the substantive issues that matter to them (the terms of an agreement to revise the job description to one that fits or to secure the resources they need, for example) a parallel discussion—or *shadow negotiation*—is taking place simultaneously. The shadow negotiation is where parties tacitly negotiate over how in fact they will negotiate. Dealing successfully in the shadow negotiation requires the use of three other major types of strategic moves:

- *Positioning moves* are the steps a negotiator takes to get into a good negotiating position, something especially important for those with a tendency to get in their own way. These moves include taking stock of one's value in a negotiation and recognizing where one is vulnerable, benchmarking to get good information (closely related to gathering intelligence as we describe in Chapter One) in order to feel more confident about asking for what one needs, and developing alternatives should the negotiation not succeed.
- *Power moves* are the steps a negotiator takes to get reluctant or more powerful parties to deal seriously with issues. These entail making

---

*Note: To protect privacy and ensure candor, aside from those who appear in published accounts, we have disguised the names of the women who appear in our stories, although we quote them, and have masked the identities of their companies.

one's value visible and finding ways to raise the costs of the status quo either alone or by enlisting allies to help.

- *Appreciative moves* are actions a negotiator takes to enlist the other party to join in the problem-solving process. It involves understanding and respecting others' good reasons for disagreement and finding ways to build on their ideas as well as yours.

In addition, *Everyday Negotiation* equips you with ways to manage the situation when others use power moves to put you on the defensive. The book covers the use of *turns* that reframe the situation, such as interrupting the move, naming it, correcting it, questioning it, or diverting it. Turns enable negotiators to continue to advocate for their needs when the other party pushes back.

Joining the principles of the shadow negotiation with the insights about what leaders need to negotiate for, the stories in this book carry substantial lessons for anyone—male or female—trying to puzzle through the changing landscape of today's organizations. The women in this book had a good idea of where they wanted to go when they took on new leadership roles. But they remained flexible regarding the ways to get there. Often the game plan evolved as they drew others— top management, peers, and reports alike—into a dialogue. In significant ways the stories reported here demonstrate the importance of relational work—soliciting different perspectives, inviting others to join the decision-making process, but clearly articulating the end goal throughout. What started out as *their* initial problems—the target of their change agendas—became a collective enterprise. And in these ways, they negotiated their place at the leadership table.

CHAPTER 1

DRILL DEEP

Negotiating the Intelligence
for Informed Decisions

It is a truism that information is a prized asset in today's complex, often matrixed organizations. Few leaders would launch any new project without careful preparation, yet they frequently take on high-profile assignments optimistic that they can make them work once on the job. By contrast, in overwhelming numbers, the women we talked to who successfully navigated difficult and visible new assignments counted good preliminary intelligence among their most valuable tools. Drilling deep not only enabled them to determine whether the role was a good fit for them, it also helped them negotiate the conditions of success before they set foot in their new offices.

Moreover, these leaders went after a particular kind of intelligence. By and large they took for granted their command of market trends or the competitive landscape, the technological edge a new product would enjoy, or the distribution channels the company needed to develop. That expertise they counted as part and parcel of any leadership position. As the head of procurement for a Fortune 500 manufacturing company put it: "The hardest part in a leadership role is not the work. That's easy if you are halfway smart. It's the ability to read the political tea leaves."

Good intelligence allows the new leader to put those tea leaves to work. Seldom did the successful women in our sample approach new roles confident that they were a perfect fit for the job. Rather, they assumed that the role itself was negotiable and probed for what would tip the odds of success in their favor. Sometimes they tested the breadth of support behind the initiatives they would be charged with spearheading. Other times they used their intelligence gathering to get past the rhetoric and identify future obstacles.

The successful leaders moved quickly to get a handle on the problem they were charged with solving and the expectations circling round its resolution. A high-tech executive offered a promotion to straighten out the company's back-office operations used her networks and one-on-one interviews to discover how deep the troubles went.

> The order process had broken down. Receivables were in awful shape. Salespeople were having a fit because no one could figure out their commissions. Financial controls weren't working. It was a disaster.

Armed with that intelligence, she could approach the CEO and accept the assignment—subject to one condition. She would need time to do the job he wanted done. "When things are in that much of a mess in finance, it's usually because processes have gone amok. There aren't quick fixes."

Most of all, the women who seamlessly managed the transition to new roles focused on unspoken codes of behavior and the personal dynamics at work in key relationships. Many new leaders are promoted from within or recruited from outside because something needs to be fixed. Indeed, this is more likely to be the case for women.[1] Not everyone in the organization, however, will be ready to accept the need for new leadership. No matter how elegant a proposed plan for, say, turning around a faltering division, gaining competitive advantage, or revamping outworn systems, it will find its way to the circular file if it rubs against the organizational grain or fails to garner critical support.

Early intelligence can flag how deep the resistance to change goes and where potential alliances might be formed. When, for example, a human resource executive contemplated joining a rapidly growing construction firm, she had no doubts about her ability to transform an organization that was essentially still run as a mom-and-pop operation. Even though the culture no longer correlated with where the company was on the growth cycle, many of the old guard liked things the way they were. The key to her success lay in determining whether she would have the space to make the changes necessary. Discussions with the president about his vision for the future provided that key. Growth on the scale that he anticipated demanded major restructuring.

It is clear that good intelligence puts a leader in a better position when negotiating the parameters of a new role. Yet women do not always operate with good intelligence. With limited access to the process that led to their appointment, they might not even know why they were chosen for the job. Without that information, they may make assumptions about the fit that influence not only their decision about accepting but also their perspective on what it would take to thrive in the new role.

Good informants are hard to come by when you're being recruited from outside, but even being a current employee does not always provide easy access to information nor guarantee its reliability. Women frequently find themselves excluded from key decision-making networks within their own firms.[2] Simultaneously insider and outsider, their perspective on any new assignment is inevitably colored by past experiences and past relationships. While a true outsider may be positioned for greater objectivity, being an outsider means facing the formidable task of developing reliable sources of information. Whatever the circumstances, the more you know about a new role before taking it on, the greater your chances of success.

COMMON TRAPS

Access to intelligence can be a challenge for women, yet sometimes unwitting steps prevent them from learning as much as they can about a prospective role. From the stories women told us we have isolated four key mistakes that can lead women (and men) to narrow the range of issues they consider when assessing a new position—with unfortunate results. In different ways, the traps short-circuit the search for additional intelligence. By casting an opportunity in black-or-white terms, they reduce the incentive to search out the nuanced information or multiple perspectives that lead to an informed decision about whether to take on the role. They tempt the unsuspecting to leave unexplored issues that should be put on the table for negotiation. The power of these traps shows up in the frequent refrain: "If I'd only known then what I know now . . ."

- "Fit doesn't matter; it's performance that counts."

Some people underestimate the difficulties that can be encountered during transitions into new roles.[3] Casually assuming that they will fit in once on the job, they can downplay the impact of the organization's culture and fail to appreciate the inextricable link between their eventual success and perceptions of their suitability. Others in the organization have to feel that the new leader's style is in sync with organizational norms, and they judge qualifications through that filter. This maxim holds whether the new leader is promoted from within or recruited from outside. New leaders run into trouble when they screen out signals of a bad cultural fit as noise.

Kelly, attracted to a strategic marketing firm because of its cutting-edge methodology and its span across industries, took over a struggling account in the automotive industry. A self-taught marketer, she casually assumed that if she delivered results nobody would care that she did not have the proper pedigree. With a great deal of sweat and little support, Kelly turned the account around and the client into a staunch supporter. "Then they brought in a strategy person from Harvard who had worked at one of the premier consulting firms to take over." The company wanted the account turned around; she was right on that score. But it was also inordinately concerned with its image. That preoccupation surfaced early in the ever-so-slight condescension and patronizing tone Kelly detected during the interviewing process. But she never pursued these signs and never negotiated a safety net tied to performance. "I didn't have a big school name or the proper consulting credentials. . . . He's now running a well-oiled machine that is churning out revenue that I developed."

New leaders are not always judged solely on their performance. Intelligence about the strategic business needs driving a particular assignment may not be enough. You have to probe deeper into the organization's underlying norms and values. Ignoring dissonance on this front can prove costly.

• "This is such a wonderful job; I'd be a fool not to take it."

A role can present such a big step forward in responsibility that intelligence is deliberately not gathered. The opportunity looms so large that it overshadows any need to investigate the downside. The CEO of a neighborhood health plan put the matter succinctly: "I wanted the top job. I didn't want to hear anything that would discourage me." Unfortunately, potential problems do not disappear with the suppression of evidence. They simply go underground where they cannot be worked through.

A prestigious title, a company with instant name recognition and credibility, greater authority—all hold out a seductive promise: "This appointment means I've finally made it!" With rose-colored glasses firmly in place, it is easy to overlook the hard work ahead and to skimp on gathering the intelligence that makes that work possible. Sheila managed the direct sales efforts to attract first-time investors to her financial services firm. Having grown up at the company, she felt a tremendous loyalty to it, but she worried about her future there. The company, following an industry-wide trend, had shifted its growth strategy to focus on institutional investors, and her department was rapidly becoming an orphan, with little visibility and decreasing impact on the bottom line. Sheila felt stuck. Then she got a tantalizing call from a recruiter. Would she consider a move? A discount brokerage firm was in the process of acquiring a trust company to expand its customer base. The move would put Sheila where the action was—with high–net worth clients. After watching her department lose influence, she jumped at the chance to work on the side of the business that everyone watched.

Sheila failed to gather intelligence that would have been hers for the asking—the high rate of turnover among associates and burnout among key executives at the discount brokerage. Without that intelligence, she could not negotiate for the kind of training and development that would be needed to stem the outflow of associates or for the safety net that would provide her some security in the pressure-cooker environment she was thinking about entering.

Blinded by excitement and challenge, it is easy to overlook the things that will block you. The benefits of an opportunity can, of course, outweigh the obvious negatives. The important thing is to take on an assignment aware of the downside. By drilling deep you can get past the sales pitch. Rather than ignore or suppress the bad news, let that bad news contribute to an informed decision and provide the foundation for some serious negotiation.

- "I love a challenge; I can't wait to tackle this problem."

Successful people are often optimistic, convinced they can tip the odds in their favor by sheer will and energy. Before charting the dimensions of the problem they will face in the new role, they naively assume that they can make it better. "That's an interesting problem; I can solve it."

An executive in health care insurance relished the high-risk profile of turnaround situations or problem areas.

> It's a challenge to get in and fix something. The upside to fixing a problem area far outweighs going into an area that is status quo, which everybody thinks is fine. If things are going well and you come on board and change one thing and it messes something else up, everybody says, "Uh, oh."

Zeroing in on the risk profile of a potential assignment is a key part of intelligence gathering. But this analysis tells only half the story. Interesting problems do make for interesting jobs. Problem solving, however, is seldom a solitary undertaking. Cooperation and resources are integral components of success. Focus only on the work—the *what*—and you might uncover the intellectual challenges ahead. But in all likelihood you will miss significant roadblocks. Intelligence on the *how*—how the work will get done and how much support it will enjoy—is equally important.

Caroline, a biotechnology executive with enviable connections within the venture capital world, discovered the high cost of the fix-it syndrome. Wanting to be where the action was in small-molecule drug development, she left a top-tier biotech firm to take a position with a small start-up. The prospect of helping to build a company from the ground up was intoxicating. "I thought I'd be able to fix the problems and turn the company around. I saw some warning signals, but I ignored them."

Caroline took it for granted that—after twenty years in the industry—the company's founders knew how to "form and structure a business." She excused some questionable practices as a lack of business sense. That she could supply. "They were spending money on frivolous things like a logo. They were paying consultants way too much for stuff that didn't need to be done." Caroline was sure she could fix that. Not long after she walked in the door, she realized her optimistic assumptions had been overly generous. She had overlooked some serious issues.

> The founders didn't lack business sense. They knew exactly what they were doing. Their friends worked for the companies that they were giving business to; they were buttering each other's bread.

Fixing problems is basic to leadership positions. But more is involved than coming up with a brilliant solution. Some problems prove more intractable than expected not because they are inherently more complex but because the organization lacks the collective will or the resources to solve them. However tantalizing the problem, it is a good idea to temper the fix-it syndrome with concrete intelligence on the problem's prospects for solution.

- "I don't have much choice; I have to take this on."

A lot of situations can make you feel boxed in. Perhaps your company is going through a merger and you would be grateful to land anywhere. You may have spent a long time with your firm and have a gloomy view of your prospects elsewhere. You may be at a point in your career or with a company where second chances are few and far between. Turn down a promotion and the powers that be will think twice about offering another. In an era of downsizing, mergers, and increasing pressure for more productivity, there may not be much room at the top. Pass up an offer and another will not necessarily come along. Our stories are peppered with vignettes from women who thought they had no choice.

The assumption becomes problematic, however, by extension. Little perceived choice on the initial decision can subconsciously translate into no choice at all. The assumption frames the decision making in categorical terms—Yes, I will accept; No, I won't—and forecloses the possibility of "Yes, but" or, better yet, "Yes, and." Even when you do not think much of your bargaining position, there is almost always room to maneuver. Taking on an assignment—accepting that *no* is not an option—does not mean that there are no other options to negotiate. However constrained the initial choice about taking on the role, there remain multiple points that can be negotiated on just what that role entails (and will need).

Karen, a veteran with a Fortune 100 consumer product company, was asked to take over integrating the R&D functions after a merger. "The role was difficult. The guy there was a caretaker who couldn't wait to get out." But Karen did not think she had much choice at that point and accepted the assignment. Trapped by feelings that she could not say no, she never drilled down to find out whether there were negotiable elements. The job might have been reconfigured to mitigate the difficulties ahead.

It is fine to recognize the perils of saying no in various organizations or of passing on an offer from a new firm. The danger comes in thinking that a *yes* carries across the board and forecloses the possibility of negotiating the terms of that acceptance.

STRATEGIC MOVES

Digging deep can help you stay out of your own way. The intelligence it yields makes for more grounded decisions. But, more than that, it sets the stage for a process of negotiation. Turning down an opportunity because it seems too much of a stretch forfeits that opportunity. Good intelligence can surface the information you need to negotiate and see whether the job can be reconfigured to work for you and the organization.

To be effective as a leader, you need a role that is aligned with the organization's needs and with your goals. Difficult assignments are easier to take on when they come with support and a safety net. All those conditions can be negotiated. These negotiations never come with a fail-safe. You can never be certain that they will produce the desired results. But they might. That is why drilling deep is so important. The intelligence often reveals the issues that must be negotiated and provides ample clues that can help you put together your strategy. As one of the women observed: "If businesses could afford it, everyone would date before they got married. All you can do is to find out as much as you can."

Drilling deep for the intelligence keys on people—likely dissenters as well as supporters—and breaks down into four linked strategic moves.

- *Tap into networks:* The more you know about the situation, the better prepared you will be to negotiate the conditions of future success. Using your networks, both internal and external, is a prime way to gather broad-brush information. It gives you multiple perspectives on the opportunities and the difficulties ahead. It can also produce useful thumbnail sketches of the people involved.
- *Scope out the possibilities through engagement:* The relationships you create with key individuals and stakeholders are critical to effectiveness.

Engaging with them helps you test whether you can work together productively and begins the process of role negotiation.

- *Confront confusion:* Intelligence gathering can produce contradictory impressions. When things are not hanging together, when mixed messages keep coming, pursue those contradictions. If consensus is missing on the assignment, it is a good indication that difficulties lie ahead.

- *Anticipate blockers:* Support for a new leader is never universal—nor is resistance. Identifying potential blockers early enables you to develop a strategy for dealing with them before they gain momentum or sabotage your efforts.

Alice Lind, a broadcasting executive, was recruited to head up a major division of a media conglomerate. Alice wanted any assignment she took on to be a win for her and for the company. To decide whether this move was the right one for her, she drilled deep for intelligence. As she uncovered more and more information, she used it to negotiate with key people to create the conditions that were likely to make her effective in the new role.

Alice started her intelligence campaign with two criteria in mind: First, she wanted a boss who did not micromanage—"I wanted someone who hired really good people and then got out of their way. I had worked in the past for some aggressive borderline personalities with punitive leadership styles. I didn't want to go there anymore."

Then she hunted for signs that the organization gave more than lip service to the standard lines about creating learning environments. "Everyone says that. You have to test the rhetoric."

We return to Alice after the discussion of each strategic move in this chapter and trace her steps as she searches out information to learn enough so that she can negotiate a role that will work for her and for the organization.

Tap Into Networks

Nothing substitutes for good information, but that information can come from a number of sources. Networks represent a major resource and can provide particularly useful help when it comes to analyzing choices. Successful women leaders tend to maintain two different types of network: a strategic one usually made up mostly of men who can advise them on their career and work, and an equally strategic network of women they turn to for support and advice on choices and challenges.[4]

Because networks are made up of individuals, their members have different perspectives, and those insights can expand your thinking about a new role or position on two critical levels. First, network members' familiarity with the organization can help you get behind the sales pitch, which may gloss over potential problems with, say, the resources that will be available to you, or the company's reputation or market share. Second, the process of interacting with key players, if candid, can provide valuable clues on the tenor you might enjoy in your working relationships once on the job.

Learn About Challenges from the Inside

People within the organization may have held the position or a similar one in the past. These are the people who can give you a better understanding of the role. Those who have been with the organization for long enough can also offer important observations on the organization's norms and culture as well as the prevailing style of its key leaders.

Even before Barbara began serious discussions with her boss about her potential new role as a deputy managing partner, she spoke to others in the firm about their experiences in similar positions. The role of deputy managing partner is a complicated one in Barbara's firm. First, the majority of deputy managing partners are women, but the managing partners they report to are men. Given these reporting relationships, Barbara worried about her ability to create and maintain a portfolio of work that she could claim as her own. Since the position was limited to a two-year term, she needed a body of independent work she could point to later.

To gather intelligence on this thorny issue, Barbara mobilized her women's network within the firm. From their responses, she spliced together a good picture of how female colleagues managed their relationships with managing partners and differentiated their work. These discussions gave Barbara, already a very senior woman within the firm, the intelligence she needed to negotiate not only the space and the support she needed to take the lead on a strategic firm-wide project but also the recognition that went with it.

Mobilize External Networks

It's also possible to build networks of people who hold similar positions outside the firm. They can serve as benchmarks against which to evaluate a role. These benchmarks make it easier to defend and justify what you need in the upcoming negotiations.

Gloria, about to be promoted to executive vice president in the private banking division of a money center bank, mobilized her networks outside the firm. Talking to women in comparable positions at other large banks, she learned about how the role was defined in those organizations and discovered the range of resources the position commanded. The resource equation included both budget and the compensation package. Gloria then put this benchmarking intelligence to work so she could defensibly ask for what she needed. In negotiations with the bank's president, she used it to back up demands for a resource allocation that fit the job. (As a sidelight, this networking paid off in another way—Gloria's list of contacts at other banks grew geometrically.)

Seek Advice from Mentors

Mentors fall into a distinct networking category. Whereas members of most professional networks focus on the job, mentors and others with whom you have maintained close relationships are concerned about *you*. Their advice is based on their knowledge of you and provides unique insights. But individual mentors furnish different kinds of counsel. Some offer primarily social and psychological support while others confine their advice primarily to career advancement.[5]

Wilma's mentor supplied both. When she was asked to shift from project leader to vice president of business development, she thought it was a crazy idea. Her mentor convinced her that she had the skills to take on the position and be effective. "I've watched you in sales meetings. You connect with the client. The rest you can learn." His advice encouraged Wilma to accept, but she still entertained doubts about the rest of the job's requirements. Before talking to her mentor, Wilma would have turned the offer down. Her mentor helped her think about what she needed to succeed. She negotiated for sessions with an executive coach and for a safety net. If either the president or she was not satisfied with her progress after a specific period, she could go back to project management, which she really loved.

Tapping into networks should involve a multifaceted approach. Marianne, a specialist in senior placements at high-technology companies, mobilized her diverse networks to evaluate an opportunity on the West Coast. Her company had its full complement of partners, and with the drop-off in technology hiring, she did not see much possibility for growth. Then a call came out of the blue from the managing partner at a much larger firm. They had an opening in their technology practice, he said, but the recruitment process was confidential. "That was a tip-off that I should investigate pretty thoroughly. I'd heard via the grapevine that there was an internal candidate, but it wasn't working out."

The managing partner took her out to lunch and offered her the job on the spot. "That worried me even more," Marianne says. Although the managing partner was charming and charismatic, he avoided offering any details. On the way out the door, he quoted a starting salary. The offer was so offhand that Marianne did not know whether it was real or not, nor did she have much sense of where she would fit in the organization. "We didn't talk titles or the profiles of the clients I would be handling."

Marianne wanted to accept, but she also wanted a clearer picture of just what she would be accepting. She began to tap into her networks for more detail on the firm and the key players in that office. Marianne started her inquiries with four advisers located in New York, rather than close to home in San Francisco. "You have to do this due diligence quietly, both to protect you and to protect your sources," she says. One of the four, a woman, headed human resources for a major media conglomerate. The woman had been Marianne's original mentor, hiring her directly out of college and then shepherding her transition to search. Marianne took her advice seriously. "This mentor had her ear to the ground everywhere."

The connection was fortuitous. Marianne's mentor had interviewed the managing partner when her company was selecting a search firm to use for a key appointment. The impression he created was not positive. "When she told the managing partner that they were interviewing other firms, he said, 'I don't do shootouts.'" Marianne's mentor considered his reaction arrogant, an attempt to circumvent the company's internal processes, and recommended another firm. This information gave Marianne pause, but she was still inclined to go ahead. She thought she could work with the managing partner and smooth out his rough edges. Her alternative—staying with her firm—was not very attractive to her.

At the request of the managing partner, Marianne met with another partner and got a formal offer, one somewhat lower than she was expecting, given her previous informal conversations with the managing partner. With a concrete offer in hand, Marianne began some serious due diligence. She called a peer in another search firm who had gone up against the managing partner on numerous occasions. Like Marianne's mentor, this peer advised extreme caution. In a business that depended on circumspection and reputation, he was uncertain of the managing partner's principles. He also thought the man could be difficult. "He told me they had a lot of résumés from people who had worked for him," Marianne says. The information was upsetting, but still Marianne was inclined to go ahead. She *really* wanted to make a move.

Finally, Marianne decided she needed to tap sources inside the firm. Although getting information from sources within the company was difficult, Marianne managed to discover quite a bit from people at the firm. She learned that the managing partner did not have a background in technology and was not a likely sponsor in her specialty. "Off the record," everyone told her to stay where she was.

Not one to rush to judgment, Marianne considered this feedback carefully. Everybody, as she says, has a "rap sheet." In tapping into multiple networks, you can sort out whether the feedback from an individual source is an outlier or represents a broad consensus. "You have to see if it's consistent," she says. In Marianne's case, it was—consistently negative. Before she started seeking out various sources for information, Marianne had no way to know that this move would have been a big mistake. She might just as easily have discovered that the opportunity was just that—a great opportunity. At a certain point, the preponderance of the evidence signals you to bow out gracefully or pursue the assignment aggressively.

Alice Lind tapped into an extensive network in media and communications that she had built over time. "You need to talk to a lot of people who know the person you are going to work for. Because you know what you don't want, you have to know how to ask the right questions in a way that people will respond and reveal things. What is his management style? What are the communication requirements? How often do you talk? If you had to name one thing that drives you crazy about this boss, what would it be?" She sought out colleagues who knew the chairman. She interviewed them. "I even asked the chairman for references." And then she talked to them about him and his style.

Alice was also concerned about the culture in the firm. She wanted to work in a collaborative environment where decision making was widely shared. She looked for indications that the company supported training and professional development. In her experience, that support was a key indicator that employees were valued. During interviews with the head of human resources, she asked about in-house training support—"How much money is spent on training as a percentage of budget? How does HR work with each of the operating units and deal with the people issues? What frames compensation? Do you benchmark against other companies and other positions? What is the turnover rate?"

Alice also networked both inside and outside the company to get a handle on the company's reputation. "I got a heads-up on what people felt were, from an industry perspective, the opportunities and challenges ahead for the business." All this intelligence informed Alice's perspective when she began serious negotiations with the chairman about her role.

Effective networking yields feedback on a position but also on your qualifications to take it on. It helps you get a fix on why you are being considered when other candidates might seem more appropriate choices. It helps you answer the critical questions—Why are they considering me? and Why are they considering me *now?* It opens your eyes to what it will take to be effective in the role.

But how do you know when you have learned enough? It can be tempting to gather so much information that it becomes paralyzing. As one of the women confessed: "I learn so much, I see all the reasons why I shouldn't take the risk that the new role entails." She misses the point of gathering intelligence. The information points out what you need to negotiate to mitigate as much of the risk as possible.

Scope Out the Possibilities Through Engagement

Networking provides general and comparative information. Engagement, by contrast, enables you to drill deeper with individuals with whom you will work. In interview after interview, the women stressed the importance of establishing solid working relationships with colleagues and superiors. These stakeholders have different personalities, different ways of communicating and making decisions, different biases. Can you work together productively? How strong is this one's commitment to the job you are taking on? Does that one value what you bring to the table?

Some critics contend that women put too much emphasis on relationships—that performance is *all* that matters. The women we interviewed uniformly disagree. They have learned that their effectiveness is inextricably bound to the strength of the relationships they are able to form. Nor do they assume that they have special skills as women that make these relationships any easier to build. Connecting with others—on problems, on roles, on mutual interests—takes work. People do not always share what is on their mind, particularly when someone new is coming in or a change on the organizational chart is contemplated.

Test the Match with Your Skill Set

The most productive intelligence gathering happens when the information flows both ways. You need to know as much as possible about an opportunity before taking it on. But you also want to make sure that the key players involved in the decision are making it for the right reasons. They have to value what you bring to the table. Credentials and experience seldom line up exactly with the requirements of a prospective assignment. Rarely are the dynamics perfect. The key questions intelligence can answer are whether you can be credible in the role and whether the expectations are reasonable for both parties.

By engaging potential colleagues and bosses, you do more than learn about their styles, their modes of operating, and their interests. You create an opportunity for them to get to know you—your abilities, approach, and objectives. In other words, you both advocate for your own interests and connect with these critical players.[6]

Establishing value can be pivotal if you are recruited from outside or do not bring the usual credentials to the assignment. New leaders are always under close scrutiny and it is imperative to discover whether perceived gaps in expertise are likely to cause headaches later. When Lisa joined an information technology company with 130,000-plus professionals worldwide, she knew next to nothing about technology. Her previous experience had been in government and international finance. She was brought on board to rescue three large (and visible) contracts. She drilled deep with software designers and the firm's management, intent on finding out why they would choose her. She discovered unanimity on the need. The firm was revamping the Medicaid processing for three states and the project was in chaos.

"All three clients were worried." The firm's reputation was on the line and they needed someone who realized the importance of getting it right, but also who could talk to the clients. Without that intelligence Lisa doubts that she would have accepted the position, let alone been able to negotiate with the engineers and management to get their commitment on the time and resources she needed to rescue the projects.

Eager to ferret out information about a prospective assignment, you can focus all attention on the intelligence coming in. It is easy to overlook the importance of sending information the other way. The preliminary steps you take to establish your value during an intelligence campaign lay the groundwork for mutual respect to develop. At a minimum, the effort ensures that all parties are comfortable with the potential fit.

Test for Gaps

Scoping out through engagement is a mutual testing process. You are interested in probing how key stakeholders understand the difficulties and opportunities ahead and whether that understanding connects to yours. As the discussions unfold, you can assess whether they see potential gaps in your credentials. Are those perceptions likely to impede your effectiveness? Are they strong enough to interfere with the benefits you hope to realize from the assignment?

Teresa kept a firm hold on her objectives when she joined a state insurance commission. She brought the academic credentials of an MBA and five years as finance director of a high-profile nonprofit. She also knew that she did not have star power, and the commission operated squarely in the political arena.

Teresa pressed the commissioner on her lack of connections and political savvy. "I was not a political animal. I was not connected. I didn't know any of the players." At each point he reassured her, playing down the commission's political sensitivity. "He sold the commission's independence." But Teresa's skepticism was aroused. "I didn't get a good feeling though—there were too many unanswered questions."

Teresa suspected that she was not the ideal candidate. Subsequently she discovered that she was the second or maybe third choice. But she weighed the information and decided to accept the position anyway. The important point is that she went into the situation with her eyes wide open. She wanted to move out of the nonprofit sector. This opportunity, even if short-lived, would give her experience in public finance and credentials as a CFO, and it would broaden her contacts significantly. And she felt that working with the commissioner would be a good learning opportunity.

Test for Chemistry

Through engagement, you create occasions to explore specific issues. But you can also use these opportunities to test for rapport. The tenor of the conversations reveals a good deal about the possibilities of working together productively. Emily, for example, had twin goals in her intelligence campaign. After working abroad at senior levels for large firms in the telecommunications industry, she wanted to return stateside and land a position where she could contribute to growth over the long haul.

When Emily was recruited to take over human resources for a spin-off telecommunications company with an international footprint, the pressure was intense. "The IPO was looming. The CEO kept saying, 'We really want to move this along.'" Emily slowed him down, and he responded favorably to her careful coaching. That, she thought, was a good sign.

> The environment was chaotic. The growth was phenomenal. But it's one thing for a job to be exciting and interesting; it's another to get in there and have the whole thing collapse.

Only by engaging key individuals was Emily able to figure out whether the job was doable and would create the opportunities to contribute that she sought. She singled out relationships with the management committee as the critical indicator of her ability to be effective.

> My gauge was whether I could develop a rapport with them within an hour to the point where the discussion could turn from me telling them my background to how we would work through a couple of issues. So you are already on a platform that assumes, "We're colleagues; we can help each other through this process. It is not going to be easy, but we can figure some ways we might be able to move this thing forward rather rapidly."

Emily was not content with scoping out the possibilities for rapport, however. She probed decision making and priorities.

I also tested how open the key individuals were about the tough issues, especially the people conflicts within the organization. Again looking at the role that I was considering, I needed to understand if there was going to be a possibility of building a team.

During each engagement Emily took care to demonstrate the value she would bring to the organization and her ability to deal with complex contractual issues. These meetings also helped her figure out what she needed to be successful in the role. To contribute at the level she knew was within her reach, she had to secure certain commitments from the CEO. Although the previous incumbent had been a vice president, Emily's experience as an ex-pat convinced her that titles were important in the global arena, especially with an IPO in the offing. She needed to come on board as executive vice president to have parity with her European counterparts. She also needed parity at the home office. Human resources had to be considered a full-fledged member of the executive committee. The title would secure that membership. The CEO, already engaged and anxious to bring Emily on board, agreed.

Opportunities can be tested on multiple levels during an intelligence campaign. You want to figure out where the prospective assignment fits with your long-range plans. But you should be equally concerned with discovering whether you want to spend a lot of time with these particular people—whether you detect in your interactions with them the promise of solid working relationships developing in the future.

Test How the Role Is Defined

Engagement lets you test chemistry. It is also the primary vehicle for negotiating revisions in the way a role is defined. What's offered is not always a good fit. Alternatively, it may be a good fit, but not something you want to be doing. Or worse, as currently configured it seems like a recipe for disaster. There is always potential room to modify a role to fit your career aspirations and in ways that make your life more livable as well.

Demands that encroach on your personal life do not have to be accepted in their current form. As you gather intelligence, you can explore how much flexibility there is and whether, with some deft negotiation, the role can be reconfigured. Helen, one of the most senior women in technology sales in her Fortune 100 company, would be the first to admit, "You never turn down an assignment in my firm." But within that corporate constraint, she leveraged her intelligence to move beyond that categorical "yes/no" and negotiated terms that made a new role attractive. "The two previous incumbents were pushed out for nonperformance. Top management wanted someone who knew global distribution channels cold." Drilling deep, Helen discovered "that someone was me."

Helen, the mother of two teenagers, did not relish spending the next three years on airplanes or in the firm's foreign subsidiaries. She had enjoyed a great career with the company and did not want to risk being forced out if she did not accept the offer, which she considered a real possibility at her level. After much thought, Helen came up with a solution: she could put her mastery to work in the home office if she had the right lieutenants. They could gain valuable experience and accumulate frequent flyer miles, and she could spend more time with her family. Her knowledge of the company told her to position this demand not as a lifestyle choice but as a needed team-building effort. By negotiating terms of an ostensibly nonnegotiable offer Helen produced an alternative that was good for everyone: key staff members got important experience, the quality of Helen's home life improved, and the company saw its channel distribution in capable hands.

Alice Lind singled out the relationship with the chairman as pivotal to her decision. Having had some bad experiences in the past, where she felt micromanaged and sometimes abused by bosses, she wanted to discover whether she and the chairman had the makings of a good working relationship. She had specific criteria in mind. She wanted a relationship that preserved her autonomy, but one that also made him comfortable.

Alice and the chairman spent many hours together. Their first encounter was over the telephone, and even there she felt a positive chemistry. "He's much younger than I am, and I brought experiences to the role that were different from his. The conversation was easy." It was clear to Alice that their styles were complementary. "I'm a pretty broad thinker and so is he. As the conversations unfolded, one question would go off into dialogue as opposed to question after question. We had agreement on the important issues confronting the business." They were also comfortable with each other. "I was authentic. He was authentic. There was no posturing. The energy was good. And that was the way it was—easy, comfortable, but invigorating and fun."

In their ongoing conversations, Alice began to engage him on her role and the way he envisaged working together. "After interviewing with the executive committee and with certain intelligence under my belt, I could go to the chairman and say, 'This is my preliminary assessment of this role. These are the kinds of things I would need from you in terms of resources.' That's when he could have said, 'I hear you, but forget about it.' So there were now ways to move [the conversation] from the possibility of a partnership to concrete ways of working."

As part of that negotiation, Alice posed situations where she would need support and tested to see if it would be there concretely. "I told him there would be a need to reevaluate the entire team. My guess was that there were people with baggage who might not be able to make the turn, given where we both wanted to see this business go. He was going to have to support me when it came to making tough people decisions." The chairman agreed that the team Alice inherited might not be the one to move the company forward. When she did have to make these tough decisions later, she had his full backing.

Conversations about the job and business take place whenever a new role is in the offing. It is what happens in these conversations that is important. Through engagement, the successful women in our stories tested their intuitive reactions, listening not just to what was said but to the tenor of the talk. They paid attention to the information they were receiving and to their feelings. They trusted their responses to the quality of the dialogue and to the participants. This scoping approach enabled them to use the conversations as the first steps in building relationships critical to their future success. As part of that relationship building, they were revealing the value they would bring and also the style they would use. They demonstrated both as they began to negotiate the terms of their future role.

Confront Confusion

If scoping out through engagement is about initiating critical relationships, confronting confusion is about surfacing and exploring potential difficulties. Confronting confusion starts with intuition. In the conversations you've had, things just do not seem to make sense.[7] The mixed messages create a vague sense of unease. For good reason. When the main story line does not hang together, the contradictions often reveal a lack of consensus on the role as well as the obstacles ahead.

Not all the i's can be dotted and the t's crossed up front when a new assignment is contemplated or a new role considered. A certain amount of confusion is natural. As a result, people often ignore these signals, figuring that they can take care of them once they are on board. That can be a dangerous approach. Not all confusion springs from superficial sources. Beyond a certain threshold, the confusion, if not confronted, can seriously reduce your effectiveness. Top management's ambitious plans do not square with the organization's capabilities. How can you perform without the basic systems in place? The CEO balks at putting you on the operating committee, but promises you free rein. How can you exercise that authority if you don't have a voice at the table? Is this a setup?

Pushing back on disconnects like these—confronting the confusion—brings potential misunderstandings out in the open. By paying attention to these mixed signals, you can get to their source and begin to negotiate toward a shared understanding.

Negotiating this shared understanding up front is particularly important because an expectation of change accompanies any shift in leadership. These days new people are invariably brought in to fix problems, but before taking on a problem, you need to know why management thinks you are the person to fix it. Otherwise you will not be able to negotiate the support you need to carry out your mandate. You also need some clarity on the problem's dimensions. By confronting any confusion here, you can negotiate the expectations of just how far-reaching the changes must be.

Confront Confusion Over the Reasons Behind Your Selection

Confusion can start right off the bat, with you. You may not be sure why you have been tapped for a key position. You may not know why you are being considered or why you are in the running at this particular time. A disconnect on the talents to be marshaled on a new assignment can mask a more troublesome confusion on the role itself. For example, when the management committee of a major consulting firm drafted Rebecca—an energetic partner—to take charge of a faltering region, she admits, "I was shocked, to be honest." Given her track record as an effective team builder, Rebecca naturally assumed she had been singled out for her people skills. But over the years Rebecca had also acquired a reputation for her willingness to deliver a tough message—to top management and team members alike.

Rebecca was not, in her words, "an unvocal person." She quickly moved to clear up the confusion, pushing back on the reasons for her appointment. As she expected, "The word *teaming* figured high on [the] list." But so did her ability to make hard personnel decisions. "The word *tough* was used about forty times, I think." Probing, pushing back, Rebecca discovered the complex reasons behind her selection. This intelligence helped her understand what the new role demanded and what the management committee expected.

Confront Confusion Over Commitment

New or expanded initiatives can create confusion over the level of commitment needed to get them off the ground. Conversations focus on the results—the addition to the product line, the increased revenues, the smoother operations—with scant attention paid to what it takes to get there.

Polly confronted this confusion when the president of a public broadcasting station approached her to lead its largest fundraising drive ever. The plans were ambitious. But were they realistic? Warning flags went up for Polly when she noticed that no one on the board talked about the additional capabilities and infrastructure that would need to be put in place. She pursued the mixed messages aggressively, quizzing the board and then key staff members, the president, and even the volunteers.

At the end of one meeting I asked the staff members to send me the operating plan and list of top donors. There was dead silence. One person said, "Well, I guess we could call the finance department and get them to pull something together."

As she suspected, the infrastructure would not support the drive. The development department did not generate its own data. Every time she needed a report, she would have to run to finance.

Polly confronted the confusion directly with the CEO. She pointed out the chasm between the development office's capabilities and the challenging campaign ahead. Something had to give. They could muddle along as they were, in which case she would pass on the job. Or they could commit the resources needed to pull off the campaign. With the right systems in place, she estimated that they could significantly raise the target. The CEO—a "terrific guy"—apologized. He was so excited about bringing her on board for the campaign, he just assumed she would "take care of the backroom stuff." Confronting the confusion between aspirations and capacity head-on, Polly not only got the commitment she needed, she also brought the CEO to a greater understanding of what a major campaign entailed.

Confront Confusion Over the Role

And, finally, confusion over how a role is defined must be confronted. Lines of authority or responsibility can be blurred, giving rise to both mixed messages and dissension over the boundaries.

Catherine confronted these conflicting views when she was asked to take over as interim CEO at a credit union. An executive vice president when the previous CEO left abruptly, she knew that the board had been struggling. Relations between the former CEO and board members had turned sour. Unappreciated, they began to intrude on day-to-day operations. With no shared vision of what corporate governance entailed, the board concentrated on details. "Members," Catherine says, "were not only unpaid—they were unhappy."

With board members unclear on their responsibilities, Catherine's role was left in limbo. To address the confusion, she bought a copy of John Carver's *Boards That Make a Difference* for each board member. Carver's model of board governance provided an objective third-party perspective as they began to define the separate roles of the board and the CEO. During these discussions Catherine paid attention to group dynamics and made an effort to solicit individual points of view. "I spent a lot of time pre-selling my ideas." Clearing up the confusing notions about respective roles had two outcomes: The board was happy and pressed Catherine to take the top job on a permanent basis.

Alice Lind tried to identify what she called "potential disconnects" between her view of the business and the chairman's. "I had gotten a heads-up from people I knew in the industry about the challenges and the opportunities. I wanted to see whether the chairman saw the same challenges. Was there a disconnect between, say, how the advertising community viewed the business and how he viewed it? Since I would be interfacing with the ad community, I didn't want to have a big disconnect." Talking about the advertising budget and target audiences convinced Alice that she and the chairman were on the same page.

Alice did have to push back a bit on the structure. The company had operated in the past as a "consortium of free-standing units." The chairman was comfortable with the current structure, but Alice felt it would have to change. To her, the functions were interrelated and she believed they needed greater integration to move the company forward. Without that integration, Alice's efforts to forge a productive interface with programming and marketing would have been frustrated. The chairman was reluctant to restructure. Over several conversations, Alice tried to understand his hesitation, but she also began to explore the comparative costs and benefits of the two organizational charts. In the end, she persuaded the chairman that integration would not only save the company money by eliminating duplication, it would make for more efficient operations.

By confronting confusion, you surface potential problem areas that can then be negotiated through. You want to start any new position with as little misunderstanding as possible to lessen the chances of unpleasant surprises.

Anticipate Blockers

It is a good idea, when taking on a new role, to remember that organizations are political places—and that the people in them are political players. They have interests to protect and agendas to advance. They also operate with mixed motives—concern for the organization's health and their own career being the prime drivers. There will always be outliers whose ambition swamps all other considerations, but in the main, executives' corporate and personal interests pull in the same direction. Or at least they almost always think they do.

Notions about the best course for an organization to follow, however, can diverge radically from one executive to another. As a general rule, it does not matter *what* future agenda you are associated with, your appointment will run into opposition from those who believe it interferes with their interests—corporate *or* personal. An influential division group president subtly pushes for her candidate. A colleague, sensing a rival, lobbies against any new initiatives without specifying the one you are in line to head up. A subordinate whose career tracks that of his boss lobbies behind the scenes.

If initial attempts fail to block the appointment, the disaffected often try to undercut the newcomer once she is on the job. They question whether she will be strong enough or has the organizational clout to turn around the operation. They cast doubts on the agenda and her ability to see it through. They withhold information or tie up the release of needed resources with red tape. Meetings mysteriously get rescheduled, or the newcomer is excluded from them.

Individually these spoilers can cause trouble. When unchecked, they can foment dissension and spark the beginnings of a blocking coalition.[8] It is essential that anyone taking on a new position anticipate who the potential blockers might be. Early identification prepares the way to negotiate a truce or to work on other means of neutralizing their impact. Resistance and naysaying, if allowed to persist, can undermine early efforts and make a tough new job even tougher.

Identify Probable Blockers

People block for what seem to them good strategic reasons. They may have little interest in your success if they see their influence waning as a result. Passed over for the position, they may harbor resentment. Alternatively, they may sincerely believe that the choice does not bode well for the company. Other candidates, in their mind, would have been able to pull the team together or been more effective change agents.

Gina faced this challenge when she was promoted to vice president for technical services. Not an engineer by training, she anticipated that the software engineers would question her appointment. "Even though I have a computer sciences degree and a background in the field, there would be grumbling. 'Why wasn't I chosen?' 'Why wasn't our beloved engineer given the job?' "

Going into the role, she knew that she would have to contend with potential blockers. She monitored behavior and productivity, looking for clues as to the likely candidates. They were easy to spot. Based on this intelligence, Gina set out to neutralize them or, if possible, convince them to come on board. The carrot she used was proof that those management skills they thought insufficient qualifications for the job actually made *their* jobs easier. "My strength is in management; my technical background supports the management decisions I make."

Gina's intelligence also told her that the grumbling had been going on for some time. "The engineers felt marginalized by my predecessor. He's abrupt and makes decisions by fiat. He was almost always right, because he's so smart, but the engineers felt that they had no say in their jobs." Intelligence not only pointed out possible blockers, it showed the way to convert them to supporters. Gina began right from the start to involve the engineers in the decision-making process.

Look for Likely Sources of Resistance

During reorganizations, the new roles created usually reapportion responsibilities. Some people emerge with expanded functions; others find their burdens lightened. Since influence links inextricably with responsibility, not everyone will embrace the changes. Typically they react by resisting. Although the resistance can be public and direct, more often its expression finds less obvious outlets. Anticipating the behavior enables you to put a strategy in place that either enlists the potential blockers to work with you or minimizes their opportunities to influence others.

Emma stepped into a newly created position as development director for a prestigious liberal arts college. Emma's role, the result of reorganization, fused previously separate functions—corporate and individual fundraising and alumni affairs. The rationale behind the change was clear. The school wanted to work more closely with alumni to expand its fundraising base. The idea was to mobilize devoted alumni so that they would not just increase their giving as individuals but would become partners in development.

Emma, recruited for her background in development, had no credentials in alumni affairs. The associate director for alumni affairs, however, was experienced. She could clearly run the function effectively while Emma devoted her attention to upgrading the fundraising office. Fundraising was understaffed, but Emma resisted the temptation to bring on another associate director immediately. Over the course of several conversations with the associate director of alumni affairs, Emma realized she could easily turn into a blocker and undercut Emma's efforts to build the new department. The woman managed her department well and enjoyed a comfortable and long-standing relationship with the associate dean. She would resent any attempt by Emma to insert a new layer of leadership between her and the dean. With this intelligence, Emma proceeded carefully and cemented her relationship with the associate director before making any moves to increase the management staff in fundraising. By then, instead of undermining Emma's decision, the associate director actually supported it in talks with the dean.

Pick Up on Who Might Be Disaffected
Some people block because they have been denied the promotion they consider rightly theirs. In other situations, potential danger comes from individuals who have been eased out of a position for performance

reasons, but remain in the organization. And occasionally an incumbent sticks around ostensibly to teach a successor the ropes, but cannot resist the temptation to second-guess.

Andrea faced this prospect when she considered a move to a quasi-public state finance agency as CFO. The demands of the financial function had outgrown the skills of the current CFO. A long-time political appointment, he was taking early retirement. After helping Andrea get oriented, he was slated to leave the agency. "The notion was that with some tutoring from him, I'd be fine."

During the interview process, however, Andrea realized that the transition might not be so smooth. "The director treated the current CFO, an older gentleman, as a father figure." Andrea could see the problems with how the financial function was run. Those she could handle. What concerned her was the current CFO. He had the director's ear. Watching the director's deference to the CFO during those interviews, she decided that she would never gain his confidence if he heard a running commentary on her actions and decisions from someone else. And the CFO was someone, she thought, who could not resist meddling. She would need the director's commitment that the tutoring period would be of a specified—and short—duration. Andrea was in a good position to make this demand since the financial function needed a thorough overhaul and she had the expertise to make it happen.

Figure Out Who Feels Threatened

Finally, blockers can be expected to emerge when a newcomer's agenda threatens their interests—either organizational or personal. Beverly, as head of human resources, had witnessed the phenomenal growth of the construction company where she worked. Five short years transformed it from a local outfit to a publicly traded regional home-building powerhouse. The president, well aware that the organization's structure had not kept pace with its growth, asked Beverly to take charge of administration. "The sticking point was whether I could get people to accept me in this expanded role." The president's plan increased

Beverly's responsibilities—but not her authority. She would still report to the vice president of finance. And he would jealously guard against any effort at greater autonomy.

When Beverly headed up only human resources, "all hiring approvals had to go through my boss in finance." She was "always caught in the middle—the person communicating back and forth." That arrangement would prove untenable if her responsibilities increased to all administrative decisions. The vice president of finance, however, would fight any move to change the reporting relationships. "Everything the other executives wanted would cost money and he was the money person. He enjoyed having the final say."

Beverly imagined the likely reaction of the other executives: "Why do we still have to go through finance? What's the point of dealing with Beverly if she can't make the decisions?" She also expected that the vice president of finance would undermine any attempts she made to deal directly with other members of the executive team. To be effective in the new role, she needed to neutralize his ability to undercut her. "Finally I talked to the president. I explained that this triangle effect was time-consuming and not in anyone's best interest [conveniently sliding over the opposition that would come from finance]. If we didn't change the reporting relationship, there was no point in carving out a new administrative function. It would fail." The president agreed. The vice president of finance would likely remain a potential blocker, but Beverly had negotiated up front the support she needed to deal with him.

Alice Lind faced a potential blocker. In the interest of putting all the revenue units under one roof, one of the division presidents would now be reporting to Alice instead of the chairman. "This was going to be a really big give-up for her. Having run a business myself, I could understand how hard this would be. During the interview process, I told her that." Alice described the interview as difficult and emotional. "She is my contemporary. We both knew that we were telling the truth about how hard that was for her, how I would have to prove to her that I would support her initiatives and not divide her team." They have since become business partners.

Anyone taking on increased responsibilities can expect resistance from people who see their interests compromised by the appointment. But those blockers can be identified. Dealing with them early on is a challenge. Sometimes they can be enlisted as potential partners. But that conversion is not always possible. When it is not, a new leader needs to act on that intelligence and use it to circumscribe their influence before they can assemble a blocking coalition.

❖

Drilling deep provides the information you need to make informed decisions. Greater understanding of the factors in play lessens the temptation to cast situations in black-and-white terms. *Yes or no* gives way to *maybe* and opens up the possibility of negotiating other options.

The women we interviewed who engineered successful transitions acted on the intelligence that they gathered in various ways. But one aspect remained constant. The intelligence oriented their subsequent negotiations. Some, after exploring the risks, used the information to negotiate a safety net. Wilma, for example, gave up a job she loved to take on business development only after she had negotiated the possibility of a return to project management if neither she nor her boss was satisfied with her results. Teresa, on the other hand, used the information about a difficult situation and a difficult boss to calibrate whether a new job as CFO would answer her personal goals, even if her tenure turned out to be short.

With each increase in awareness, each layer of information, these women added to their ability to bring new opportunities into alignment with their leadership styles and personal measures of success. They probed and pushed on the resources they would need, the backing they could count on, and the criteria by which they would be judged. They explored the reasons behind their appointment—the skill sets and experience they would be expected to bring to bear. But they did more than uncover this information; they used it as a stepping-stone to negotiate resources, to clarify metrics, and to forge the beginnings of good working relationships. They tested for chemistry and commitment;

they engaged in a mutual exploration of the problem they would be charged with solving.

These efforts at drilling down enabled them to approach their new situations with their eyes wide open. They saw the possibility of stretching the current view of the role. Helen, now head of channel marketing for a major technology firm, used her knowledge of corporate culture to broaden her choices beyond a nonnegotiable yes-or-no decision. Roles are negotiable; you can make them fit your needs and those of your organization. But you have to know what points need to be negotiated. Intelligence provides those insights.

KEEP ON PROBING

Digging deep for intelligence is, however, not a one-time thing. There is a limit to what you can know before actually taking on a new role. Pushing for certainty where none is available can create the impression that you are high-maintenance individual. As key relationships evolve, roles must be constantly renegotiated. Situations change—new leaders come in, restructurings occur. With each change, the steps of drilling deep need to be revisited.

> Alice Lind, for example, explicitly contracted with the chairman for reality checks going forward.
>
> "The culture here is driven by being nice but not necessarily honest. I said to him, 'Part of why we are going to be a good team is that I have had some experience in facilitating change, but you are going to have to tell me how fast and how far.' There are times when I have told him that [the troops] were getting a little uncomfortable. Am I moving at a pace that's too fast? He told me to keep on, but keep an eye out.
>
> "This culture and my boss are also big believers in feedback. He gives it to me and I give it to him. We share. That has been helpful as a newcomer to an organization. It's taken me thirty years to figure it out."

In a world of rapid change, adaptive power becomes a critical factor in organizational success.[9] Good intelligence is a cornerstone of adaptability. At no point, perhaps, are adaptive powers stretched more than when considering and taking on a visible, high-profile assignment. Good intelligence makes the initial decision and the transition more manageable. It puts you on alert when a key relationship may need to be shored up and signals the appropriate time to push for more support. It also helps you understand the reasons behind resistance. Moreover, intelligence is a renewable resource and drilling deep a perpetual process.

GET READY TO DRILL DEEP: STRATEGIZING TO NEGOTIATE FOR INTELLIGENCE

Effectiveness in a new role hinges on negotiating the conditions of your success. To negotiate, however, you need to be prepared. Only with the right intelligence can you make informed decisions. Consider what you know about yourself and what is important to you in any role you take on.

Tap Into Networks
People—mentors, sponsors, those on the inside and the outside—can help you make solid decisions. But you have to seek out their counsel. Have you tapped into your networks to gather data on the company, the key players, and the role?

- Prepare a list of questions you need answered about the role. Pay attention to your motivations for considering the assignment, issues that make you uneasy, and your other options.
- Who inside or outside the organization is best positioned to provide the answers you need? (If you are having difficulty identifying the right people, ask yourself, Who knows the people I need to talk with? Then ask that person for an introduction.)
- Who knows you well and can be trusted to give good advice? Encourage them to ask you challenging questions about why you should or should not relish the assignment.

- Is there a pattern in the information that you don't want to acknowledge? What is it telling you—about the personalities involved or the histories of your predecessors?

Scope Out the Possibilities Through Engagement

Success in any role is more complicated than simply doing a great job! You will have a hard time enjoying the work and performing to a high standard if you do not enjoy solid working relationships with your peers and key players in the organization. Have you engaged them in meaningful conversations about their expectations?

- What business and organizational issues do you need to discuss with key players? What do these discussions indicate about your chances of establishing good rapport with them?
- Does your style complement theirs? If not, how might that complicate your working relationships?
- Does the role as described fit your needs? What modifications can you propose? If you do not think you are in a position to turn down the assignment, how much flexibility do you have in defining it?

Confront Confusion

Is there anything that seems confusing to you? Are you getting mixed messages? Trust your instincts. If something seems odd, you need to ask more questions.

- Why have you been selected for this assignment? Are your experience and skill sets a good fit? How serious are any perceived gaps?
- Are you getting mixed signals about the firm's commitment to the business objectives or to your appointment?
- Do you have a clear mandate? Is there consensus on the problems? How committed are the key players to fixing them? What will it take to get their commitment?

- Do you feel comfortable that you understand the parameters of the role? Where do you fit on the organizational chart? Are there any disconnects between the descriptions of the role you are getting and the organizational structure?

Anticipate Blockers

Do you expect resistance? You should. Don't be surprised. Figure out the people who might be potential blockers and think about the reasons why.

- Who might be unhappy with your appointment? Why?
- Will anyone feel threatened by your appointment?
- How can you bring them on board or at least neutralize them?
- Will you have the authority to redeploy or replace them if their resistance becomes destructive? Have you enlisted key players to still doubts or blunt outright opposition?

CHAPTER
2

MOBILIZE BACKERS
Negotiating for Critical Support

Intelligence pays off. The more you know about the business and political challenges of a role, the more confident you can be about making it work for you and the organization. Unfortunately, this optimism is not always universally shared. In any competitive environment, there remains abundant room for skepticism. Not everyone in an organization will be willing to give you the benefit of the doubt or suspend judgment until you have a chance to prove yourself.

And in that uneasy period before performance—the proof— kicks in, the questions about fitness and legitimacy for the role can be intense. In fact, 68 percent of the senior women we surveyed at a professional conference believed that their success was *not* presumed when they took on prominent roles. Their experience showed them that their leadership skills and abilities were likely to be more closely scrutinized than those of their male colleagues. Under the microscope, constantly tested and then retested, they placed a high premium on proving themselves. Only then could their hopes of success be realized.

What is remarkable about the results of this informal poll is that one-third of the women did not expect that questions would be asked. Unprepared, they may not have recognized how important first impressions can be. Nor would they have been in a position to appreciate how their ability to perform could be undermined or their authority to lead questioned. In failing to anticipate the scrutiny ahead, they may have passed up opportunities to negotiate the breathing room they needed or the backing that would channel the testing in productive directions.

One of the women was candid in her appraisal: "After three months, I want people to say things are on the right track." Such endorsement cannot be taken for granted. You need help in making it a reality. And that help starts at the top. In the process of drilling deep, you engage key stakeholders to probe their commitment to the task at hand and their confidence in your ability to handle it. That commitment and that confidence need to be mobilized to influence others in the organization.

Leaders are constantly measured and constantly tested when they take on new assignments or expanded roles. They are expected to produce, but to deliver results they have to be in a position to make that performance possible. This situation creates something of a paradox for new leaders. In order to lead, they first have to be perceived to have the authority to lead.[1]

Myriad business and political factors come into play in building confidence in an appointment—whether the newcomer is male or female. As discussed in the Introduction, with today's rapidly changing environments, new assignments are rarely a perfect fit. New roles clearly build on past accomplishments. But they also create challenges for the future. As others assess an appointment, they can focus on achievements or they can concentrate on the gaps and what is missing. You may have some experiences that are exactly on target. Maybe you have managed several large technology projects and heading up the unit seems a logical next step. Sure, you delivered discrete projects on budget and on schedule. But others in the organization may question whether you have the technical expertise or the financial background necessary to lead the enterprise. When Dick Parsons tapped Pat Fili-Krushel to be executive vice president of administration at the newly formed AOL TimeWarner, she was an unlikely choice in many ways. The company was in crisis; as Jeffrey Bewkes (now CEO of TimeWarner and then CEO of HBO) described it, it was World War III. With a distinguished career in media, Pat had been president of the ABC network, but this role was a staff job. When Parsons offered it to her, she asked him if it was an HR job. Parsons wanted her because her line experiences would give her clout with the CEOs of the divisions. However, many of the HR leaders in the divisions were not pleased that they had not been offered the opportunity. As a result, working with them through the HR Council to promote her agenda became a challenge.[2]

Because the fit between person and role is seldom perfect, the take on that fit will always be subject to conflicting evaluations. When Hillary Rodham Clinton was nominated by President Barack Obama as secretary of state, there were some who said her selection was merely a political move to bring in a "team of rivals."[3] Negative "press" compromises the new leader's ability to claim authority in the role. Without that authority, leading others becomes almost impossible.[4]

All leaders are subject to scrutiny, but, as discussed in the Introduction, the questions about a women's legitimacy and experience can be especially focused and intense. It is here that backing from key leaders is crucial. Whether key backers are countering faulty rationales against an appointment or just putting their credibility behind their choice, they are an invaluable resource. But such backing is never a given; it must be negotiated, and certain conditions can make those negotiations more or less of a challenge. When relationships go back a long time, a new leader can usually count on the backing of senior people. The top executive in a large manufacturing company summed up the situation up well:

> When I put folks in a leadership position, I don't let them fail. I know them; I've mentored them and given them opportunities to prove themselves over the years.

This executive's confidence in his appointments grew out of the rapport he had established with up-and-coming managers. Because his relationships with male managers tended to be on a stronger footing than those he maintained with the company's female managers, he had less hesitation in putting men in leadership positions and backing those decisions. For the women, the situation was more complicated. He did not know them so well—their relationships were more recent and more tentative. Before making those appointments, he needed additional convincing; in his mind, there was still some testing to be done. This executive had not even a scintilla of bias against women. In fact, he actively championed their participation at the highest ranks in the company. But the women could not automatically count on his support; they had work to do to negotiate for his backing.

COMMON TRAPS

Newcomers can hesitate to mobilize the backing they need for many reasons. They may feel compelled to prove their worth and tackle the job without asking powerful allies for help. They may underestimate the testing ahead or the doubts their appointment will raise. They may take it for granted that the title carries adequate authority. Tantalized by the problem they are charged with fixing, they may concentrate on its complexities and let important relationships slide. Or, not surprisingly, they may get so caught up in their own concerns that they overlook the legitimate worries others might have. Whatever the reasons, they close themselves to opportunities to start the new assignment off on the right footing—with key players engaged and solidly behind their efforts. And they do so at their peril.

Three traps, in particular, get in the way of negotiating critical support. If allowed to go unchecked, they can lead to one of two conclusions, both unfortunate. The new leader taking on a visible assignment can minimize the important role key backers can play in her transition. Or, alternatively, she can underestimate the difficulty of bringing them on board.

- "My appointment speaks for itself."

With a big job in the offing, it is only prudent to try to negotiate the conditions that will make you successful. A critical aspect of that effort involves convincing yourself—deciding that you *can* make a success of the assignment. But the thought process can be a slippery slope. It is an easy slide from thinking you are the right person for the job to concluding that you are the only logical person to take it on. Pretty soon the assignment seems inevitable and any gap in experience or qualifications dwindles to inconsequential proportions.

The appointment seldom "speaks for itself"; others in the organization may mount some quiet and not-so-quiet opposition. Perhaps they do not think your credentials stack up against theirs or those of a valued mentor. Perhaps they enjoyed productive relationships with the previous incumbent and worry about disruption. Or perhaps that gap in experience does not seem so narrow from their perspective. And when political expediency cautions against articulating the real reasons behind their opposition, they easily find proxies.

Negative first reactions are perfectly natural. But they must be curbed, or you will not be able to command the authority in the role that you need to perform it. For example, when an international consulting firm promoted Carlotta, she was delighted. A star performer in one of the firm's major concentrations, Carlotta had accumulated impressive credentials in client service and business development. To her, the move to a leadership role seemed an obvious next step. Not all her peers agreed. Good performers themselves, they did not accept that Carlotta should be the one to lead them. The rainmakers among them figured out that they brought in more business. Others thought about their own happy clients.

Carlotta failed to recognize that the appointment did not automatically convey credibility. Convinced that she was the right person for the job, she never anticipated the resistance. It didn't occur to her to ask the chairman to pave the way. She was content with a formal announcement. Six months later, Carlotta was still having problems pulling the team together. Team members had little incentive to accept her leadership. In fact, the silence from top management told them that little cost attached to their lack of cooperation.

The task of providing a rationale for an appointment naturally falls to the key players in the organization who made the decision. But they may never be asked if the newcomer assumes that those reasons are self-evident. No one, and particularly not a woman, wants to take up a prime position without a credible and persuasive introduction.

- "The results are what's important."

The opportunity to work on an intriguing problem can be seductive. Often it provides that extra motivation to take on a demanding role. On the job, however, a tantalizing problem can turn into a different kind of lure. It is hard to resist the temptation to dig right in and get on with what got you the assignment in the first place—your demonstrated ability to solve problems. Credibility and authority, after all, flow from results. So you focus all your energy on a problem just waiting for a solution. Soon day-to-day pressures squeeze out the time it takes to engage key people in the new effort. When, as one of the women put it, "you are driving down the road at eighty miles an hour," it is all too easy to lose sight of the bigger political picture and let key relationships slide. A partner in a technology start-up characterized the dilemma:

> You're working hard, getting the results. You've developed fifty accounts at X companies that have enabled the firm to make Y amount of sales. You don't have the interest or the time to manage the political or personal side—or somehow don't see it as that important.

This approach poses two dangers. First, results lag efforts. Impressions, however, form quickly. Perceptions of you as aloof, disconnected or, even worse, as merely a "worker bee" without the ability to think strategically may gel before you have a chance to fix the problems you were brought in to remedy.[5] Second, results are not always immediately visible. While certain performance indicators are easily measured, others are less obvious. Jill, a financial services executive, was asked to co-chair a strategic cross-channel initiative to increase client satisfaction and to improve loyalty and retention. Not surprisingly, the relationship managers whose clients were affected were reluctant to make the introductions required. "We needed to take the time to explain to the relationship managers why we, as a firm, were taking this approach. We had to get Legal involved to check on potential client concerns we could anticipate. And we had to consider a 'product' offering that would offer value-added solutions for this client segment, which is very different from our typical client. But one of our sponsors was impatient because she wanted a big splash right out of the gate."

Building a department or a new process takes time. But beyond that constraint, progress is not so easy to define or quantify. Others in the organization may not even be aware of the accomplishment, much less give credit to the driving force behind it. Without vocal appreciation from the top, a terrific performance can, in effect, become invisible within the broader organization. With no public acknowledgment, no credibility or authority attaches to the performance or the performer. That is what happened to Julia when she was hired as CFO of a quasi-public agency.

> This was a great opportunity to step up from director of finance to the CFO role. I could see all the problems. In a quasi-public organization you have a lot of funds. They didn't understand how the money flow was supposed to work and come together. We had a million cash accounts and I helped them consolidate those and get them invested. I did lots of very concrete things to get our financial house in order. I was well liked. My reports loved me.
>
> But I never developed a relationship with my boss and his other direct reports. The consequences affected me personally. Frequently I was out of the loop. It could have been anything from a conversation at the State House that would impact an investment to the CEO's notion of an off-site retreat.

Julia accomplished a great deal in a short time. In fact, she did manage to get the agency's financial house in order—the problem she was hired to solve. Her performance, however, was discounted in the organization. It went essentially unrecognized at the top. Soon others took their cue from the CEO and his team. As the lack of appreciation spread, Julia found her ability to claim her success undermined and her credibility as a leader in jeopardy. There is only so much you can do on your own. Perceptions of performance count and they are shaped in large part by key players.

- "I don't want to seem weak."

Even in an era that extols the post-heroic leader, images of the heroic version die hard.[6] Take, for example, the negative media commentary President Obama took when he took time to carefully evaluate the decision to send more troops to Afghanistan in 2009. Real leaders don't dither around for months holding meetings where all attendees have a chance to voice their opinions.[7] Real leaders make decisions—quickly.

Requests for help can be read as a sign of weakness rather than an attempt to consider all options before making a major decision. And the coded language of gender stereotypes makes it more complicated because by definition it is women, not men, who ask for help. Any appeal by a woman runs a certain risk. It can push these gendered notions to the forefront. She's a woman, she needs help, she can't make it on her own. She is, in the words of several of the women, "high maintenance."

A request does not necessarily trigger these associations, however. Couched appropriately, it may be interpreted as a sign of strength, not weakness. It all comes down to the way in which the appeal for backing is made—to the how, when, and what.

Keisha failed to appreciate the distinction when she was appointed vice president of administration at a large research organization. The lion's share of the organization's revenues came from government contracts. Keisha's charge was to control costs and to ensure that the accounting on any given contract was above reproach. Operating in a hierarchical environment, she assumed that the job came with a mandate to institute accounting controls. "I was the new sheriff in town," she says.

Keisha developed protocols that introduced greater transparency to contract expenses. The staff members responsible for the contract work, however, were research scientists who had held significant positions in government and academia. Getting them to adhere to any policies was like herding cats. Although Keisha had some control over reimbursements, she had virtually no authority to compel the researchers to follow the new reporting guidelines. Determined to prove herself, she did not seek help in implementing them. She thought that any request would be viewed as evidence that she could not make it on her own. So she resorted to holding up the researchers' expense accounts. The triviality of this response served notice that they didn't need to take her seriously. It would be "business as usual" on the contracts.

Keisha could have mobilized support from the vice president of R&D to enforce the guidelines. The scientists reported to him, and it was in his interest to make sure that government oversight committees remained happy. The high-maintenance label usually gets applied when the appeals are continual or when the request is impossible to grant. It is unrealistic, for example, to enlist backing for a series of trivial requests or for a configuration of reporting relationships that would have negative and broad implications elsewhere in the organization. Neither criterion held for Keisha. She saw weakness in asking for help. Ironically, because she could not perform and institute necessary changes, she confirmed the impression of weakness she wanted to avoid and put the organization in an equivocal position with its clients.

The missteps that these notions encourage are all avoidable. Why go it alone when you can have help?

STRATEGIC MOVES

Impressions form quickly. Others in the organization inevitably mull over the same questions that any newcomer puzzles through when deciding to take on a new assignment. They ask themselves: Why this person? Why now? What does this change portend—for me and for the organization? How serious is management? They test to see whether the newcomer is up to the task. They push back to find out the influence she can bring to bear and the resources she can command. And in all this testing they take their cue from key members of the organization. It is incumbent on anyone taking on a new assignment to make sure that those cues are on the mark—vocal and unequivocal.

The "seal of approval" takes multiple forms, but without it the start of any strategic assignment can be rocky indeed. As a senior woman in an accounting firm put it: "I need to know that leadership has my back and that I have their continued confidence. It is important to me and to the people on my team." That support must be clear organizationally and worked out personally. Key players can begin to entertain reservations when they sense disgruntlement. By engaging them, you deepen relationships that can be a bulwark when things get rough; you also have in place communication channels to divert negative energy in more positive directions.

In drilling deep, you engage key stakeholders to probe their commitment to the task at hand and their confidence in your ability to handle it. You build on that commitment and that confidence through four strategic moves.

- *Work out expectations:* At times the expectations surrounding what can be accomplished do not dovetail with the realities on the ground. Other times, a new role comes with no established expectations, and they must be created. The objective is not only to negotiate the backing you need from key people in the organization but also to reach mutual agreement on how you will work together.
- *Secure strategic responsibilities:* A new leader's list of strategic responsibilities provides a snapshot of priorities. In turn, those responsibilities can shape perceptions of your performance and affect your visibility throughout the organization. You secure those responsibilities by negotiating with the key players involved.
- *Have key leaders make the case:* Only top leadership or the board can tie an appointment to an organization's strategic vision. They have a built-in platform to articulate what needs to be done to get the department, division, or company moving forward and why you are the best person to accomplish that task. Their agreement to

make the case must be negotiated. Otherwise they might opt for a laissez-faire approach.

- *Seed storytelling opportunities:* People in organizations talk. As they tell each other stories, those narratives become embedded in their perceptions. Strategically placed allies can help spread the good news, framing the newcomer's story in positive terms.

People have a lot riding on major appointments. As one of the senior women in technology pointed out: "If you take on a big job, you are taking a chance and the people who put you there are taking a chance. You don't have much time to make mistakes." Researchers Dan Ciampa and Michael Watkins estimate that 64 percent of executives hired from the outside won't make it in their new jobs. And those promoted from within can expect to encounter rough sledding ahead.[8] The first six months of an assignment, they contend, are a make-or-break period.

Just as we followed Alice Lind's steps as she put together an intelligence campaign, in this chapter we track Susan Vega's strategic moves to mobilize key backing behind a difficult new assignment.

Susan's firm had carved out a niche in the competitive consulting world with its focus on implementation. Susan thoroughly enjoyed the client contact and during her five-year tenure as head of the financial services practice had grown revenues from $20 million to $110 million.

The leadership at the firm, a partnership, periodically rotated, and these rotations typically produced a shakeup of the top consultants. Susan co-chaired the nominating committee for two years and participated in the selection of the new team, a stint that gave her considerable visibility. "When the new leadership came in, a lot of changes were made. I won't call it a housecleaning, but . . ."

Susan had gotten to know the future chairman during the firm's courtship of a big credit-card account. "In those meetings I brought diversity to a white male enclave and hit it off with the bankers." The future chairman, at first active in the negotiations, eventually watched from the sidelines. Susan's immediate grasp of what the client needed and her decisiveness impressed him. Two months later he asked her to take over the Southwest region.

Susan was skeptical. Her forte and passion were in client services, not administration. Other partners were less charitable. The more polite intimated that the region, with the heavy concentration of oil and gas clients, was too hard a nut for her to crack. But much of the commentary was considerably more blunt.

"I got picked because I'm a woman. The job was a payback for voting right on the nominating committee. I was too young."

Susan says that there is always that different perspective on when a woman is ready. She is forty-two. The previous chairman ran the firm at forty. She only looks young. She has dealt successfully with tough-minded bankers and negotiated fees with shrewd investment advisers for five years. But instead of dismissing the commentary as unpleasant noise and "a lot of grousing," Susan admitted its corrosive potential and set out to prove the backbiters wrong. She started by mobilizing key support within the firm.

Work Out Expectations

Backers come in many guises. They can be sponsors who recommended you for the position. They can be an immediate boss or a leader not involved with your work on a day-to-day basis. They can be board members or influential consultants. Newcomers to a position leave relationships with these key players unattended at their peril. Faulty expectations among key players can derail a new assignment. Too optimistic and they lead to disappointment. Left ambiguous, they give rise to discord. By managing these expectations actively, anyone taking on a new role increases her chances of getting off to a good start—and, with feedback mechanisms in place, of staying on track.

Just because people selected you does not necessarily guarantee you will have a good working relationship with them or that you can count on their backing when the going gets rough. These relationships need to be developed and then renewed at each stage of their evolution. Managing them in a 24/7 world is an ongoing process. Effectiveness on the assignment often hinges on the success of that process. Key leaders, by their actions and words, can buffer your transition to a high-profile assignment. Or they can leave you on your own to sink or swim.

In working out expectations, the first hurdle is bringing key players to the understanding that not only can they have a productive relationship with you, the task ahead requires it. The next hurdle is developing the outlines of that relationship—how you will interact with each other and work together. Tacit ground rules need to be established for your interactions—simple things like how often you talk and not-so-simple things like how you treat each other. Finally, a good working relationship is one built on mutuality, where each can learn from the other and both can grow.

Build Mutual Respect

Sponsors, bosses, and board members can be pivotal players as you try to claim authority in a new role. Since you need their backing, your first challenge is to negotiate relationships with them that are based on mutual regard. These kinds of relationships are not happy accidents. Nor can they be assumed. Someone may have been instrumental in tapping you for a leadership position without knowing you well or without knowing you at all. The new role may be the product of a reorganization, and you came with the package.

Getting to know potential backers is not something that happens overnight. But the process must be initiated by you, not left to chance encounters. Before you can get these relationships off on the right foot, however, you might have a certain amount of correction to do.[9] Key leaders do not always start with unbiased or positive impressions. In many cases, they don't have much of an impression at all, and you may have to establish your credibility and your credentials. That is what happened to Gail.

Gail stepped into the general counsel's role at a major metropolitan hospital after a medical emergency forced the hospital's top lawyer into early retirement. While the CEO was grateful to Gail for filling the void, he considered the move a stopgap measure. "Frankly," she says, "he thought I was a lightweight, lacking in gravitas." It never occurred to the CEO that the soft-spoken, diminutive lawyer might want the job as a permanent assignment.

Because Gail had worked in the former general counsel's shadow, her interactions with the CEO had been limited. To get any traction in her new role, Gail had to disrupt his perceptions of her. "He didn't think I was analytic enough or tough enough to make the hard decisions." Others in the organization would be quick to take their lead from him. Instead of scheduling face-to-face meetings with the CEO, however, Gail began to educate him on her abilities through a series of thoughtful e-mail messages. "That way he could evaluate my analytic abilities without being distracted by my lack of physical stature." As the CEO's confidence in her sharpness grew, his perceptions of her took a 180-degree turn. She had, he discovered, her own idiosyncratic gravitas.

At other times, mutual respect emerges from a testing process. When Joyce was promoted at a major technology company, her new role merged two jobs. The previous incumbents had been pushed out because they could not close deals.

Joyce had never worked for or with her new boss, and after a brief honeymoon, he started to test her.

> He tortures you badly until you've convinced him. He's always testing your ideas. We would have arguments about run rates and go toe-to-toe, yelling and screaming. He would advocate for a change in the mix, and I would feel strongly that it would be a mistake. I'd dredge up examples of problems from my experience. He'd shout back.

That was, Joyce says, "his way." She intuited that she needed to stand up to her boss. "I didn't fold and it worked. At a meeting recently my boss started quoting me. I thought he'd lost his mind," she says. "Of course, he never came back and told me I was right." That did not matter to Joyce. She had established her standing with him, a precondition for mutual respect and a significant prelude to securing his backing.

Finally, mutual respect can germinate in a critical moment or over a pivotal issue. Some action triggers a response. Sarah created just such an impression when she pointed out a problem in her new assignment. The managing partner in her accounting firm had charged her with growing a major piece of the business. To achieve her goals, however, she would have to draft people from other areas of the firm and many of them had loftier titles than hers. Without at least parity in title, she would not have the authority she needed. There was a hitch, though. "Nobody ever negotiated a title with the managing partner," she says. "He prided himself on his fairness. He gave titles when people had earned them, not a minute sooner."

Unless Sarah could convince the managing partner to recognize the value that she brought to the table, her reports and others in the firm essential to the success of her business objective would jump to false conclusions about the importance of the job she was taking on. Carefully positioning her arguments not as an attack on the managing partner's fairness, but as one of the things she needed to be effective, Sarah opened a dialogue with him. He found her argument compelling and agreed to change her title. But Sarah's move achieved more than just a title that fit her responsibility. The managing partner came to see her in a different light. After witnessing firsthand her adroitness in handling a difficult situation, he became an active advocate on her behalf. This was the ideal resolution and very much in the firm's best interests—but Sarah had to take the first step.

Work Out the Rules of Engagement

Building relationships with key backers is an ongoing process. However informal the discussions may be, you are always negotiating expectations just as you are constantly working out the basic guidelines for your communication. It is important to establish the when, where, and what of your interactions. It is even more important to attend to the tone of those interactions. The ground rules you negotiate must cover not just the access you have to each other and the feedback you will exchange but how you will treat each other.

Many of the women we interviewed had difficult and troubled relationships with key leaders. These were not just demanding bosses but ones who had earned their reputations for psychologically abusive behaviors. To work with them, they had to make clear—right from the start—the kind of treatment they expected (and would tolerate).

Some behavior tests the limits of what is acceptable. Different people will draw that line at different places. Those limits must be set, however, as Sachiko recognized when she was promoted to managing director at an investment bank. A mathematician by training, Sachiko was expert in econometric modeling. When the bank decided to roll out a new financial product, Sachiko was put in charge, reporting to the head trader. As she recalls,

> He's the most difficult person I've ever worked for. His other direct reports have trouble with him, but their relationships are not as tenuous as mine is. He has a way of laying into you that you wouldn't believe—bad language, the whole thing. Everybody has experienced being shut out, the lack of communication, only hearing from him when you've screwed up. I knew I couldn't work like that.

Aware of his reputation, Sachiko let him know her limits. When he started to yell, she turned the situation around by standing up as if to leave the meeting.[10]

> I told him that I thought we had come as far as we could in the conversation and that we'd get more accomplished if we met again at a later time. I had seen too many people being walked over by him. They never got his respect.

Similarly, Joyce, whose testing we described earlier in the chapter, let her boss know that no matter how deep their disagreements on policy issues, their often heated exchanges could not be aired in public. That would have been a costly loss of face for Joyce.

In today's busy world, establishing *when* you will interact with key leaders can be as pivotal as defining the *how* of those interactions. Unforgiving schedules make it imperative to set some ground rules for access. You want to reach at least a tacit understanding on how you are going to communicate and respect each other's time. As the head of the ethics practice at one of the nation's top accounting firms put it:

> As you go higher in an organization, the people are incredibly busy. When I took on this job, my new boss was busy with a merger. He was also based in New York; I was in Boston. But we sat down and talked, up

front, about how we wanted to work together. I would be selective in my
demands on his time, only pulling him in when I considered his opinion
critical. But he needed to be there when I did pull him in. To me, that
guarantee of feedback was essential.

There are also boundaries to be worked out over where the
organization's time stops and your time begins. High-pressure jobs
have a way of swallowing up all waking hours, regardless of outside
commitments. For women who shoulder heavy family responsibilities
the challenge can be particularly daunting. First, the suspicion still
lingers in the air of many organizations that women are less committed
to their work and less able to manage demanding assignments. And
time tends to be seen as an unlimited resource in organizations. The
prevailing expectation is that people will always do what it takes to get
the job done.[11] So negotiating about boundaries is a delicate operation.
On one hand, coming into a demanding job, you do not want others
in key positions to start questioning your commitment. On the other,
with heavy responsibilities at the office and at home, you must reach an
understanding with key players that protects your personal time. Even
without that conflict, you need to carve out some downtime.

A promotion thrust Diana, a marketing executive in the fashion
industry, not only into a pivotal role at her company but also into daily
contact with a demanding CEO. Before their first official meeting, he
sent her a list of topics he wanted to cover and told her to set aside at
least two hours the next evening. He'd have dinner delivered.

Diana, a working mother, prized efficient time management—even
with her bosses. She did not want to launch her new reporting relationship with a bad precedent. She responded to the peremptory summons
with a memo—along with backup data organized by product line and
market segment. The memo systematically addressed the CEO's topics.
She also told him that she had to leave at six o'clock.

Her husband was surprised that Diana would push back right after
a promotion. But, as it turned out, the information she had forwarded
answered the CEO's questions. Their eventual meeting lasted ten
minutes. This interaction, however brief, told him that Diana had

information at the ready and would not hesitate to share good news and bad in accessible form. It also signaled that she had boundaries.

Learn How to Learn from One Another

The final dimension of working out expectations is negotiating the information flow—how you keep each other informed and the feedback you each need. What, for example, does a key leader consider "being informed"? What sort of counsel do you need in order to develop in the job? The answers to these questions change over time as the relationship evolves. When a new leader first takes over, for example, anxiety over the appointment can force senior leaders to rethink previously negotiated guidelines. If they harbor last-minute doubts about the new project or their choice, they naturally tend to watch the newcomer's performance closely. This scrutiny can undermine a new leader's authority if it takes the form of micromanaging. People see top management hovering and begin to wonder if the newcomer is really in charge. The motivation behind the behavior may be perfectly well intentioned, aiming to ease the transition. Unless it is checked, however, it can create major obstacles to a newcomer's effectiveness. Pat, a systems engineer, had to push back on a key leader's attempts at micromanaging her transition.

Pat was tapped by the head of client services to oversee the implementation of the company's signature new software platform. The move was a big step up for Pat but it was a big challenge as well. Cuts in head counts during the slump in IT spending had taken a toll. The effort was behind schedule and the product filled with programming flaws. Her new boss was also a fanatic for detail. "He had to be," Pat says. "This platform could restore the company to profitability." He needed timely information, but Pat could not function with someone constantly looking over her shoulder. After some marathon sessions vetting the problems, the two came to a meeting of the minds. He warned in only a half-joking manner: "Now, don't screw it up." Pat used the moment to lay out some guidelines for their communication. "I will certainly try not to. But don't expect an hourly progress report. If I run into a problem, you will be the first to hear about it."

Once on the job, Pat was scrupulous about keeping her boss in the loop. But she also filtered out the trivial day-to-day information. The guidelines Pat established produced a solid working relationship. When Pat raised a problem, he knew it was one that she considered important. And she could get on with the job, assured that he would be there as a sounding board.

The other side of learning together is the feedback you seek from key players. Not only must new leaders explicitly contract for feedback; they have to put in place mechanisms that facilitate it. Feedback performs a vital function. It helps keep everyone on the same page and flags potential problems or misunderstandings before they get out of control. It is also an easy conduit for timely advice.

Martha relied heavily on feedback from the head of marketing to get her bearings in a new and demanding role. When she left a sales position in a large consumer products company to become a vice president of marketing at a smaller firm, she estimates she had "maybe two of the twenty or so requirements for the job." But the head of marketing encouraged her; he liked her market savvy and the way she related to customers. He promised to teach her the ropes and help her establish credibility within the organization. Convinced that he was serious, Martha accepted.

That promise did not materialize quite the way Martha had anticipated. The head of marketing traveled extensively and was frequently unavailable. "I became an incredible nag—bombarding him with questions via e-mail." Gradually they reached a mutual understanding. When he recruited her, he knew the job was a stretch; he would be there to counsel her. "He has his ear to the ground," she says, "and knows what is happening all over the company." They set up a calendar for monthly face-to-face meetings. They used that time to talk about how she was being perceived, the problems she was having (those she had identified as well as the ones he had heard about). But they also strategized on ways to improve the marketing function. It has been a learning experience for both. "He pulls me back before I fall off the abyss," she says. "He won't let me fail and everyone in the organization knows that."

> Susan Vega would have been happy spending her days serving the firm's clients in the financial services sector. "I'd have a nice place to live and be working on interesting problems with interesting people," she says. She agreed to head the Southwest region because the impact she had on the firm mattered to her. "If the executive committee thought the job was a better use of my talents at this point in time, I was willing to take it on."
>
> Susan's agreement confirmed some of the management committee's expectations. In other areas, however, it prefaced serious negotiation. Traditionally the job had a large public relations component. Susan set out to quash those expectations. "I wasn't going to be Queen of the United Way in Dallas. I would support the firm's community outreach and serve on committees. But I wasn't about to chair anything." Susan also wanted to build into the role more substantial contact with clients than it usually carried. "I told them that we couldn't do that right away. I would have to get in there and figure things out first."
>
> All the time that Susan was negotiating expectations about the role, she was simultaneously working out her relationships with members of the executive committee. She was not their only source of information about what was going on in the Southwest region. But others tended to avoid bad news and "downplay problems." One executive in particular would "take my feedback and then water it down when he presented the data to the executive committee." Susan negotiated a more direct feedback mechanism. "It was important to me that they hear my voice." The information was soon flowing both ways. "They would tell me what they were hearing and prop me up when I needed propping. We would bounce around ideas to make sure that I was hitting all the major constituencies."
>
> Susan also reached out to other key players in the organization, especially partners in the region. "Unless you deal with them directly on an issue, they don't respect you. I made myself available, giving feedback and making introductions. I never said no when someone wanted help with a client or personnel issue."

Working out expectations is an important activity in the early period of a new assignment. If you do not move quickly to define them, they will take form anyway—and probably not in the shape you want. Unless you push back on unfair treatment, you invite its continuation. Without reasonable boundaries with respect to availability, you can find steady encroachments on your private time. With no guidelines established for your communication, you risk being micromanaged. But most of all you can miss out on valuable counsel. Not only did the women we interviewed understand the importance of working out expectations, they realized they had a small window of time in which to negotiate them.

A lot of stakeholders have a great deal riding on key assignments. The pressures and demands of a big job can be daunting. They also open up an opportunity—the prospect of forming alliances with other members of the leadership team. The process can deepen or modulate your existing relationships, lay the groundwork for new ones, and change faulty perceptions that discourage key players from investing in your success. Not only are these relationships enriching, they are the source of much-needed support, buffering you from the skeptics and reinforcing your credibility.

Secure Strategic Responsibilities

When leaders take on new positions, they are sure to be told to delegate—delegate as many responsibilities as possible so that they can focus on the big picture, the strategic issues. This advice can be especially pointed when a promotion is involved. Old responsibilities must be left behind to accommodate the new. Workdays and energy are not infinitely elastic. Leaders moving into new areas often find that they must jettison certain tasks to make room for others. Keeping responsibility for a function does not mean keeping all the work, but the experience of delegating may be somewhat different for a woman than it is for a man.[12]

There is a prevailing myth that women have a hard time delegating. According to certain stereotypes, women are afraid to delegate. Perfectionists, they do not trust others to perform up to their standards. A junior partner in a mergers and acquisitions firm typifies this attitude: "When a deal is coming together, the pressure is horrendous. It's just easier to do the work yourself. That way you know it will get done right and you don't waste any time explaining." But there may be good

reasons for women like this partner to do the work herself or micromanage it. Under close scrutiny, they may sense that people are watching
for mistakes. Sponsors who put them in the role may also feel at risk and
so may be monitoring performance closely, concerned about whether
they will be able to succeed in the role. Whatever the circumstances,
there are solid reasons to be strategic as you decide what to delegate.
Strategic in this context means taking care to retain any function with a
direct impact on perceptions of you as a leader and making sure you
feel supported in doing so.

There is a saying in bridge: "Not all thirteen-point hands are equal."
The same goes for the tasks that fall under a new leader's purview.
Some are more equal than others, and it is essential that you identify
which those functions are early on and fight to secure them. You want
to negotiate with key players in the organization about the ways you are
going to work together and for the tools that you will have in the role.

It seems obvious that a person would want to retain the functions
associated with a particular role. On the face of it, you would not
expect the decisions to precipitate any friction or controversy. That,
however, is not always the case. Sponsors and bosses, anxious to
help a newcomer settle in, may suggest shifting certain functional
responsibilities elsewhere. "It will lighten your load and give you time,"
they say. Or they may not realize that the previous configuration
omitted critical functions. The former incumbent may not have been
involved in, say, pricing policy, but that function could have a strategic
impact on your performance and directly affect your credibility as a
new leader.

Keep Functions That Signal Your Authority

New leaders often bring new agendas. They are frequently charged
with redesigning programs or refocusing projects that have gone off
track. The challenge is to get people to follow them. Getting buy-in is a
complicated problem, but certain important signals always need to be
sent right from the start. People need to know that you will have a say in
the issues that matter to them—their performance review, their pay, or

other incentives. Unless you have a voice in these decisions, they may calculate that doing things the old way is a low-cost option.

When Paula was appointed controller of a business unit in a large manufacturing firm, her mandate was to increase coordination between sales and operations. The problem arose because the sales organization, with incentives based solely on revenues, would oversell, making promises on delivery that the operations group could not meet. Paula knew that she could not influence the sales organization to change its practices unless she had some control over its incentive system. In negotiations with the head of the business unit, Paula led the process to realign the compensation system so that customer satisfaction was kept front and center. With this initiative in the works, Paula demonstrated that she had what it took to bring sales into line and to achieve the broader business goals.

Convincing people of your authority can be particularly challenging in a role that is newly created. Turf issues are always in the background. Usually it is not difficult to figure out the strategic responsibilities essential to a role. Many jobs, however complex, have clear objectives and strategic responsibilities flow naturally from them. They are the tools that make it possible to meet the objectives. But newly created roles are often ill defined, and anyone taking them on must negotiate the boundaries and the strategic responsibilities that go with them. Even if people recognize the need to rebalance responsibilities, deep down they usually do not want to see their own influence curtailed. The rebalancing may not be a zero-sum game, but chances are good that those affected will view it that way.

Tanya confronted this dilemma when the executive director and founder of a nonprofit organization persuaded her to come on board as chief operating officer. The role was new and filled a gaping hole in the agency's organizational chart. The executive director, responsible for the agency's rapid growth, was spread thin. Program costs sometimes got out of hand, and reports to sponsors and governmental funding agencies were habitually late. Tanya first had to make the executive director comfortable with the decision to relinquish some of her authority.

Then Tanya began to negotiate responsibilities, but she framed the discussions in terms of hypothetical situations: What happens when there is a staff problem? How would we handle a failing program? Gradually the two came to a mutual understanding. The executive director would devote her efforts outward—to fostering the agency's public image and broadening its funding base. Tanya, on the other hand, would take care of its internal health, installing cost controls and management systems.

Agreement on paper or a handshake is one thing; how it plays out in real time is another, Tanya discovered. Within a year, funding started to be a problem. "The more nervous the executive director got about the funding situation, the more she tried to micromanage. She wanted to fire people for making mistakes."

Tanya pushed back. The agency had become more complex. It dealt with many grants organizations, all with different reporting requirements. Understaffing meant that things were falling through the cracks. Tanya recognized another moment in the ongoing negotiations with the executive director over their respective responsibilities. To manage the workflow, Tanya needed to retain control over staffing decisions. The discussions were difficult, but Tanya prevailed.

Tanya's negotiations helped the executive director make a tough transition. And by defining their respective responsibilities, Tanya also gained the confidence of the staff. They knew she was in charge of internal operations and would protect them from the executive director's penchant for micromanagement and snap decisions.

Keep Functions Directly Correlated with Results

Certain functions are more closely tied to results than others are. Which functions these are varies a great deal and depends on the specific challenges a leader needs to address. In building a new organization, for example, recruiting and hiring may be crucial. Decision-making authority may have to be rebalanced so that the final say rests with the line rather than the human resources department. By contrast, when you are introducing a change across a matrixed organization, control over implementation—even for a short time—often turns out to be the critical function. For Maria, a partner in a large consulting firm, it was pricing.

Maria, recently promoted to return a major practice to profitability, faced the challenge of correlating fees generated by engagements to the amount of work. The previous practice head had deferred all engagement decisions to the regional partner. "He hated to turn away business, so the economics of the engagement process were skewed to favor top-line growth." With little input from the practice, he consistently underestimated the demands certain clients made and sold business on a flat fee basis. "The practice was bedeviled with lemons," Maria says, "clients whose engagements invariably came in over budget and blotted performance records at the end of the year." Nobody wanted to work on these accounts; they could foul up a performance review.

Profitability and Maria's credibility turned on her ability to influence the pricing of the practice's services. Maria pulled together some telling data and shared her concerns with the regional partner. Although he stopped short of giving her veto power over an engagement, he agreed that they would make pricing decisions together. The arrangement brought budgets into better alignment with the scope of work and gave Maria's team tangible evidence that she recognized their problem with the lemons and was doing something to fix it.

Keep Functions That Enhance Visibility

Observers of organizational behavior have long puzzled over a curious phenomenon. Leaders and those who study leadership pepper their remarks and papers with references to teamwork, being part of the team, pulling together. Yet in many organizations, the agents that provide the glue are largely invisible. And they are often women. One of the questions discussed in the Introduction is the challenge of claiming value for "invisible work." Work behind the scenes—peacekeeping or mediating conflict and facilitating communication—can go unrewarded if not claimed.[13] Keeping functions that make potentially invisible work visible bolsters a new leader's position with those who may have doubted her potential effectiveness.

When Rachel moved into a position with shared responsibilities at a large government facility, she won out over some of her colleagues. Even though Rachel, an engineer with an MBA, carried the credentials for the job, strong reservations remained over her ability to lead the division.

Together she and her boss oversaw a sprawling operation, located in two buildings. The group ran the simulators and supported all the research and systems that went into experimental aircraft. About a hundred people, contractors as well as civil servants, were split between the two buildings. The branch head, whose specialty was simulators, worked out of the simulator building, while Rachel had more or less autonomous supervisory responsibility in other building, the hangar that housed the research aircraft. This physical separation made it imperative that Rachel and her boss integrate their responsibilities.

Rachel, in her words "a walkaround manager," maintained an open-door policy. The branch head had a very different leadership style. He wrote everything down and focused on policy. Over time, the two worked out the division of labor. Playing to her strengths, Rachel quickly became the face of the leadership team. The visibility had an immediate impact on the way she was perceived. As she went around, going "from shop to shop, talking to people," she used the interactions to take the group's pulse. She not only let people know what was happening, she also found out what was on their minds. When she detected friction between the hangar and simulator contingents, she moved to dispel it. These intercessions, coupled with her visible presence, gave her credibility, positioning her as the go-to person when problems arose and as a full partner on the leadership team.

Susan Vega had a dual charge when she took over the Southwest region. Growth was clearly an objective for the underperforming practice. But the executive committee also wanted to see greater emphasis on the long term. The firm had built its reputation on strategic implementation, but the partners were going after each and every opportunity. "We can't go after every Tom, Dick, and Harry in the marketplace," Susan told us. "The commitment of time is too great." Instead, teams would focus on specific target clients. Rather than run from one product to the next or from one pitch to the next, consultants were supposed to invest in relationships. The target list represented "a chain of relationships that would generate the next revenues, although they might not show up on the ledgers for a year or so."

"The tech consultants, in particular, sell products," Susan says. "They hit and run. They can run from one IT project to the next, but they still have a responsibility to the last one." The problem, Susan discovered, was that consultants worried about bringing any and all work in the door. The scorecarding—the rewards and compensation systems—had to value the investment in future clients and not just current revenues generated.

Traditionally the executive committee set consultant compensation. Susan convinced top management that acceptance of the teaming initiative hinged on realigning compensation criteria. To get the region to adopt the teaming approach, she would need greater participation in the review process. "I don't make the final determination," she says. "But I do get to say whether the balance is fair. If a consultant doesn't sell as many actual services as the guy who is running from product to product, but helps us penetrate, say, the client list in the drilling market, he should be rewarded."

Susan uses both the stick and the carrot implicit in her expanded responsibility for compensation decisions. Without tying rewards to the teaming approach, she would have engaged in an endless attempt to convince the region's consultants that she and the executive committee were serious.

The strategic importance of a given function ranges widely from one visible assignment to the next. But strategic functions share one salient characteristic—they all shape perceptions of a newcomer's authority and credibility. They are the drivers of effectiveness. You secure the specific responsibilities you need by engaging key leaders and actively negotiating.

Have Key Leaders Make the Case
The first hint of the backing you may have from key leaders appears in the information you gather about the role. That backing then

acquires definition in the ongoing negotiations over expectations and strategic responsibilities. By and large, these exploratory discussions and negotiations take place behind the scenes. Commitments are secured offline. Once you are appointed, however, your backing gets put to a public test.

Any shift in leadership ranks precipitates concerns. People worry about the impact on their careers. They question the motivations behind the decision. And they express reservations about the selection. "She's not seasoned enough to pull it off." "She's in over her head." "She's not tough enough to make the hard choices we need made."

These reactions are perfectly natural. Visible appointments come with high stakes—whether a man or a woman is appointed. Just because a clear gap appears on an organizational chart does not mean that the person chosen to fill the slot can slip in without stirring concerns in certain quarters. A new appointment may be inevitable. There is nothing inevitable about the actual selection. Working with key players, a newcomer can prepare the ground so that the concerns, when raised, lead to productive dialogue. Key leaders can position not only the assignment but also their choice positively.

Orchestrate a Persuasive Introduction

No one wants to take up a prime position without a credible and persuasive introduction. But all too often key leaders do not make this case for "why you" and "why now." They welcome a new person to the fold via an impersonal e-mail message. Or, even more problematic, they leave the introductions up to the newcomer. This laissez-faire approach unnecessarily compromises early acceptance. The silence provides little incentive for others to be supportive. In fact, when key leaders make no attempt to explain an appointment or to blunt criticism, they give potential critics free rein.

Grace, hired by the CEO of a real estate development company as his first vice president of administration, got a chilly reception when she showed up for work. The CEO had announced the appointment in a management meeting with a quick mention. He then circulated a blanket e-mail to the rest of the organization. It was abundantly clear to Grace that this minimal introduction wasn't enough.

> The rumors that were flying around were incredible. Before I got through the door, the operational heads had told their staffs that they didn't need to worry about my stuff. They didn't have to come to my training seminars or fill out any vacation or expense forms.

The firm had grown exponentially, and the infrastructure strained to keep pace. The founder-CEO created the position to bring order to the company's haphazard policies and conflicting practices. The operational heads, however, liked things just the way they were. They did not want any outsider coming in and meddling with their expense accounts or their vacation allotments. Grace knew she needed help from the CEO.

> I told him that if he wanted the kinds of changes he hired me to implement, he needed to let people know why I was there. We agreed that he would take each of the operational heads aside privately and explain, again, the reasons behind the new position. In effect, he told them to get with the program.

This vocal—and repeated—support gave Grace and the new role credibility. The confidential delivery also saved face for the operational heads, even while the message increased the stakes for further sabotage. In blocking Grace the operational heads were also blocking the CEO's plans to manage the company's growth.

Insist on Strategic Linkages

Students of leadership often draw a distinction between management and leadership. They suggest that managers concentrate on the present, on day-to-day problems, while leaders look to the future, setting goals and assembling the building blocks to achieve them. If they are reading the topography right, then key leaders have a critical responsibility when they make important appointments. Only they can tie the assignment to the organization's strategic vision. They have a built-in platform to articulate what needs to be done to get things moving and why you are the best person to accomplish that task.

A strategic linkage is critical in paving the way for you and your role. When Roberta agreed to take over the customer services division of a large mutual fund company, her boss made this connection. Roberta's appointment derived, in part, from the findings of a focus group she led on the division's performance.

> Customer dissatisfaction was high. The customer service network burned cash, yet investors had difficulty using it. Opinions inside the company were no better. The prevailing perception was that managers in customer service had country club jobs. They were all vice presidents, pulling down big salaries but with little accountability.

Roberta was not enthusiastic about taking on a division with such a tarnished reputation. But the CIO persuaded her. He had a vision for customer relationship management that he was pushing and wanted her help in making it happen. Once Roberta accepted, he prepared her way. He dispelled any assumptions that Roberta would be just another in a string of ineffective leaders by framing the appointment in terms of his mission. He aimed to harness cutting-edge technologies so that the fund's investors could count on premium service. Twice during Roberta's first year he met with three hundred company leaders and used those meetings to publicize the program Roberta was initiating.

Roberta could never have made this case. The CIO had to deliver the message that business as usual within the division would no longer be tolerated. His reputation and influence positioned him to link Roberta's assignment to larger corporate goals that made change imperative. His backing, expressed in plain terms, gave her the clout to get things going. Beyond that, it explicitly endorsed the policies she would need to implement over time. Roberta was charged with transforming deeply entrenched perceptions about the division and equally entrenched behaviors within the division. Justification for that transformation had to come from the top.

Encourage Different Approaches to Different Stakeholders

Backers have choices in how they make the strategic case. Roberta's CIO used a public forum. In that situation, the deep changes contemplated in the division required a broad audience. The organization's structure and its culture also shape the decision. In large organizations, a sponsor might make the case in stages—seeding the idea with other major players with the expectation that they would follow up with their own people. Close-knit communities may require a series of one-on-one sessions, akin to the way Grace's CEO brought his operational heads around. Cases are most successfully made when they are tailored to the specific situation rather than following a perfunctory protocol. The chairman at Jane's firm, for example, targeted multiple audiences and used multiple formats to make the case for her appointment. He gave potentially resistant players special attention.

The chairman had drafted Jane, a seasoned mutual funds veteran, to create an institutional relationship management department and professionalize the firm's control and reporting systems. Pension funds and other institutional investors were clamoring for more transparency and stricter controls within the industry, even turning to the courts to enforce their demands. So far the firm had escaped the spotlight. "Little fires were smoldering," Jane recalls. "But nothing was out of control. The firm wasn't in a crisis phase."

Before officially coming on board, Jane worked closely with the chairman. With little sense of urgency, one major player—the head of sales—had to be convinced not only that the change was necessary but also that Jane could pull it off.

> In the investment field there's an inevitable tension between sales and the client relationship people. The people in sales want to make the sale and move on to the next one.

Jane and the chairman sat down with the head of sales. They positioned the new arrangement as a collaborative one—a symbiotic relationship between the client side and sales. Not only would the new arrangement free up sales to do what it really liked to do—close deals—it would lay the foundation for expansive growth. By the time Jane took office, the head of sales was solidly behind the effort. "He had real influence with his people and he brought them around." (His approach was blunt—"Jane is here to keep us out of jail so we can make lots of money"—but it worked.)

In making the case for the role and for Jane's ability to fill it, however, the chairman had two audiences in mind.

> He had positioned me internally within the firm—starting with the head of sales. He made sure that everyone inside knew that growth brought with it serious business risk if not handled properly. Unless the institutional infrastructure was managed well, they might not even be able to hang on to what they had.

At the same time, the chairman used the appointment to send a clear message to the firm's institutional clients. He had selected Jane, in part, for her sterling reputation. In talks with institutional clients and in interviews with the business press, he stressed the appointment's symbolic importance. The firm was committed to future growth and would draft the best talent around to manage that growth. The appointment did, in fact, go a long way toward reassuring institutional investors, and their reaction, in turn, gave Jane added leverage within the firm.

Making a strategic case is not a one-time event. A key backer cannot simply applaud your qualifications or announce your appointment's strategic importance and then disappear from the scene. The message needs to be reinforced over time. For example, the CEO at Layla's company mounted a calculated campaign to support her role. The company, headquartered in India, provided end-to-end systems to a global roster of corporate customers. He recruited Layla to ensure that Wall Street and the analyst community had timely and accurate information on the firm's growing presence in a niche market. The role was central to the firm's prospects. An IPO was planned, and the amount of money raised would directly affect R&D and marketing budgets moving forward.

Layla was part Indian. This heritage gained her some credit in the home office. But she was based in New York, where she had the contacts essential to her role. Without the CEO's active intervention, it would have been easy for the geographically dispersed staff to shrug off her requests for market share and sales data or to discount the critical work she was doing. Instead, she enlisted her boss to help her gain authority for her requests.

> He sends out frequent reminders about the importance, to an India-centric organization, of developing good relations with Wall Street. Whenever I make a presentation at an analyst meeting, he circulates an update.

In advertising Layla's accomplishments, the CEO validated her, and this vote of confidence in turn made her job easier.

> Initially Susan Vega and the executive committee were not on the same page on how to introduce the teaming approach or her to the Southwest region. Usually the firm followed a time-tested protocol and conducted one-on-one interviews with each of the consultants affected. In this case, however, Susan pushed the executive committee to make an exception.
>
> In their view, the region was in such bad shape that the consultants wouldn't know what they needed. Whatever they asked for, we wouldn't be able to give them. More to the point, they would fight the remedies we envisioned for poor performance.
>
> Susan resisted this call, arguing that it would generate unnecessary animosity and make her job even harder. She pressed for a more auspicious introduction, and they reached a compromise: a dinner for all the consultants assigned to the region.
>
> Susan was scheduled to attend, but at the last minute had to back out because of a family emergency. Her absence turned out to be a good thing. Because she wasn't there, the chairman and the vice chair could explain, quite frankly, why they had picked her. "Apparently, they got the message across," she says. And they did not hesitate to reinforce it. At timely moments, they reiterated their confidence in Susan and the necessity of the changes she was in the process of implementing.

The backing of key players cannot be left behind closed doors—that is, left to the expectations and strategic responsibilities worked out in private. At some point, these leaders must give public voice to their support. Their influence carries weight within the organization and can mitigate opposition. But, more important, only they are positioned to connect the assignment to the organization's broader goals and make the case for why you are the best person to get the job done.

Nor is securing backing a one-time thing. Situations occur where you need to renegotiate it. As the new executive vice president for administration at AOL TimeWarner, Dick Parsons charged Pat Fili-Krushel, mentioned earlier, to make the people at the company feel it was one company, not a set of autonomous divisions. Based on the road trips that she and Parsons took, Fili-Krushel thought that they should have an annual meeting so that the top people in the company could get more comfortable with one another. She developed a plan for a one-day business meeting in New York for the top 150–200 executives. Parsons encouraged her, but others did not. She vetted the idea with all the CEOs, but just two weeks before the meeting, she got a call from one of the CEOs she knew very well. He said to her, "Pat, you've had a very good career up till now. If I were you, I would start distancing myself from this meeting because it is not going to be pretty." Fili-Krushel went to Parsons, wondering if they should cancel it. He said, "You've got really good instincts and I think this is right—let's go get them." She asked him if he had her back and he said yes. It was tough, but the subsequent meetings have been the most successful the company has known.[14]

Seed Storytelling Opportunities

All the moves to mobilize backers aim to build perceptions of you as a credible leader with the authority and legitimacy to get the work—whatever it is—done. Those perceptions are given voice by the stories that people tell about you in the early days of your tenure. One of the participants in the informal survey we noted at the beginning of this chapter was on the right track when she described a three-month target for acceptance of her status and policies. Of course, you want people to believe that what you are doing is okay. But situations can be confusing in the early months. Chaos, rather than order, can reign. There is a great deal of uncertainty. If stories get told that exaggerate the uncertainty or publicize the chaos, your ability to get the situation under control may be constrained. Some leaders never recover when the doubters overwhelm the supporters. Of course, key leaders can set a tone. Their backing makes outright opposition more dangerous and can convince fence-sitters to give you the benefit of the doubt. But you can add weight to the case they make. If you seed opportunities for people to sing your praises, you create a positive atmosphere even before results start to come in.

Find the Swing People

Any organization has its opinion leaders. Maybe they are people who have been there for a long time, the ones who hold the organization's history. Maybe they are people who float easily among various groups. Often, these influence-makers do not reside at the top of an organizational chart, and yet they can be uniquely placed to spread the word. One of the women talked about the need to have *swing people*—individuals who are networked throughout the organization—on board. Despite explicit and frequent explanations of the rationale behind an appointment, confusion can linger. Friendly voices at various levels of the organization and from the outside can provide a different kind of reinforcement from what the major players supply. They can tell your story for you.[15] That story can focus others on the appointment's positive aspects or persuade them to withhold judgment. You can even call on the storytellers to counter persistent criticism.

Andrea signed on for a leadership role in state government. She knew that the first few months would be chaotic.

> You want to draw a curtain around that chaos. You don't want people to know about it. You want their first response to be: "Boy, Andrea really whipped the department into shape."

Soon after Andrea moved into her office, she identified a few well-connected people who could be her eyes and ears. Good listeners, networked to multiple layers of the political and business communities, they reached out to Andrea's "customers." They backstopped her and gave her unfiltered perspectives, which she might not have elicited in personal interviews.

> People want to be associated with winners. So you need to encourage that perception. The rumor mill needs to suggest that things are going well. You want people to say it as often as possible—you can't spread the word yourself. You need others—those swing people.

Depending on the type of organization and your role, these swing backers can be colleagues or junior associates. They may have worked with you in the past, on volunteer projects, or as consultants. For their stories to gain any traction, however, they must be credible advocates, well-respected people to whom others listen. When, for example, Elena Kagan (later appointed by President Obama as solicitor general and nominee for the Supreme Court) took over as dean of Harvard Law School, she became the school's first female dean. It would not be an easy place to lead, and Kagan had been on the faculty only a short time. Martha Minow, one of the law school's most distinguished faculty members and later its dean, wasted no time in countering the doubts being expressed. In an interview with the local press, she openly supported Kagan's appointment: "Many of us are just delighted to be going to work at the law school right now."[16]

What is revealing about Minow's story is that she told it less than two months after Kagan's appointment and before the start of the fall semester. It was credible not because Minow had had an opportunity to canvass the faculty, many of whom were on vacation, but because she had worked with Kagan and was generally acknowledged to be a person who picked her words carefully.

Win Over the Skeptics

Swing people, disposed to think positive thoughts about you and what you are doing, tell stories from a favorable slant. Equally powerful are stories that come from people who initially resisted your appointment.

When Hillary was hired to take over the labor practice at a rival law firm, not all the partners were enthusiastic. One partner was particularly cool; he had expected to lead the practice. Although he had worked with Hillary on several cases, he never congratulated her, avoided her in the office, and made disparaging offhand remarks about her appointment. He repeatedly rebuffed Hillary when she broached the issue of their working relations.

Hillary, however, remained on the alert for any opportunity to engage him. An opening came when a highly skilled junior threatened to quit. Hillary knew from the trial schedule that her reluctant partner could not afford to lose this expertise. She offered to help convince the junior associate to stay with the firm (including freeing up money for a raise). Working with her on this shared problem, the reluctant partner saw Hillary's leadership in a different light. In short order, he became a vocal supporter. Just as he had not hesitated to spread disaffection, he was equally forthcoming about his "amazement that Hillary was doing such a good job." As word of his unexpected support spread, it nudged fence-sitters off their perches and gave other blockers considerable pause. *Hillary must be doing something right,* they thought, *if she could turn her former foe into a fan.*

Converted blockers or fence-sitters add a different dimension to the stories told about your accomplishment or leadership. Their accounts are all the more powerful because they come from previous skeptics. There is no way that they can be discarded as spin or glossed over as being unreliably biased toward the positive.

Create a Campaign

Individual stories can remain isolated—scattered about. Seeding stories requires a campaign, a sense of who tells the story, who listens to whom, and who can spread the word. Bettina, the head of a corporate foundation, found that when multiple sources told the same compelling story, they generated excitement about her foundation's work.

> Making the argument in nonprofit work is not easy. There is no return on investment that shows up on the income statement. There is, however, a social return on investment that comes from relationship building.

Bettina looked for stories that would link the foundation's funding with concerns of the corporate parent's customers. An opportunity came with a phone call from the head of the United Way. She wanted to bring Success by Six to the city and she wanted Bettina's parent to do the corporate underwriting.

Bettina strategized with partners, colleagues, and community leaders. The story spread by word of mouth and press releases. It resonated on all fronts and generated the momentum to get the project off the ground. Within a short period, the project had become a platform for Bettina's future work. It symbolized the foundation's commitment to the community and responded to a prime concern of the corporation's customers—quality education.

> When Susan Vega took over the Southwest region, certain people in the organization questioned the appointment. She was too young, not seasoned enough, not tough enough. Susan had strong networks within the firm, but it turned out that she did not have to tap them. They came forward without being asked. Members of the Women's Caucus talked about her accessibility and fairness. Other colleagues—male and female—talked about the merits of the teaming approach. Susan's experience in the financial services practice and her style, they said, made her an ideal candidate to implement the new program. They pointed to her track record in bringing in new clients and establishing long-term relationships with them.
>
> These stories, coupled with top leadership's firm backing, got Susan off to a good start and created a positive counterbalance to the resistance she encountered during her first months on the job.

❖

Early impressions matter when you are taking on a new role. Unless you have positive reinforcement from the top, negative perceptions can congeal into entrenched opinions and block any progress. Key players can influence the way others in the organization view you and energize them for the task ahead. As these backers demonstrate their confidence in you, that confidence spreads. When they lay out the strategic reasons for your appointment, others come to see the importance of the assignment and why you were chosen.

There is one final way in which key players help when you assume a new role. Their willingness to spend political capital on you and the role they want you to take on is a good indicator of the importance they attach to both. That in itself is a bolstering thought when faced with a challenging assignment. You know going in that the work has value and that you can have a positive impact on the organization.

GET READY TO MOBILIZE BACKERS: STRATEGIZING TO NEGOTIATE CRITICAL SUPPORT

You need strong backing behind you to take on a demanding assignment. Don't be tempted to minimize the impact key players can have or underestimate the difficulties of bringing everyone on board. You cannot take anything for granted. You can, however, negotiate!

Work Out Expectations

Solid working relationships with key people are not accidents. Unless you negotiate guidelines for your interactions, the relationships may get defined by default.

- What will be considered an unqualified success? By you? By your boss? By other key stakeholders?
- Do key players seem convinced that you are the right person for the role? Do they think you have the right skill set and the right experience? If not, how can you persuade them?
- Are you and key people on the same page in terms of the results they expect and how soon they want to see them?
- Are guidelines in place for your communications? How often? In what form? How much information do they need? How much feedback do you want? Are those expectations reasonable or do you have some revising to do?

- Have you negotiated (tacitly or overtly) the boundaries you need in order to balance your work and your private life?

Secure Strategic Responsibilities

Focus your time and effort on the things that matter. Strategic responsibilities have a direct impact on visibility and success. Remember, only you can prevent role erosion.

- Do your responsibilities involve work that the organization values? Can you link your functional responsibilities to concrete business objectives? Or do you need to negotiate a different mix?
- Do your responsibilities reflect your priorities? Are there some that you can offload?
- Do you have control over functions that create incentives for others to support you? That reinforce your authority? That make your contributions visible?
- Does your authority mirror that of your predecessor? If not, why not?
- Have the functions under your control kept pace with the role's expansion? If the role is a new one, have the responsibilities that go with it been clearly defined?

Have Key Leaders Make the Case

Unless the major players involved in making the appointment provide a clear rationale for your selection, others in the organization will jump to their own conclusions. Coach the key players on what they can do to pave your way. You do not want to be left to sink or swim.

- Have you recognized that your title or position may not be enough to supply the credibility you need?
- How are key players planning to announce your assignment? Who should make the announcement? When? In what forums?
- Are key leaders prepared to underscore the assignment's strategic importance? Will they explain why they chose you to take it on?

- Have they been primed to step in if the message needs reinforcement? Have you taken into account the time lag before results kick in and negotiated support during that critical period?

Seed Storytelling Opportunities
The talk in the office can either help you or hurt you. Recognize its power and actively manage it.

- Who are the swing people—the ones with influence across the organization? How should you approach them? What do you want them to say or do?
- Who are the skeptics that others listen to? How can you win them over?
- Who would benefit from knowing about the work you have been doing? Who should tell them about it?

CHAPTER 3

GARNER RESOURCES
Negotiating Key Allocations

G ood intelligence helps you make informed decisions about a new role and guides your negotiations over its requirements. Commitments first worked out in private with key stakeholders, when given public expression, present you as the right person to take on the assignment. But your efforts to position yourself effectively cannot stop there. In the early stages of a new leadership role it is equally important to pay attention to the raw materials—the resources—you will be able to command for the job. Resources—be they financial, human, or simply time—are necessary on a purely practical level. You need them to get the work done.

In a perfect world, big jobs would come with the necessary resources. Unfortunately, that situation seldom holds. Pressures for greater productivity and bottom-line results mean that resource allocations must be deliberately negotiated. As a top executive in technology sales points out: "People always ask you to consider whether you could do more with less." Resources directly impact results and by implication shape perceptions of your ability to deliver. "You can get frustrated," she says. "You begin to feel as if you are underperforming even when you are actually performing on a much higher level on a per-unit basis, since you are getting better results with reduced resources."

Given the intense push to maximize how resources are used, not uncommon in today's economic environment, you must not only negotiate the levels of support that will be available but also correlate that allocation with the results that can be expected. The issue at hand is not necessarily a question of more but of finding the right mix and linking that mix to broader strategic objectives. Rather than attempting to do more and more with less and less, you can use the allocation process to set priorities.

The resources you can garner have more than practical implications, however. They also carry symbolic significance. Any new appointment puts careers at risk. In calibrating that risk, people make their judgments to a great extent by what they think the newcomer will be able to deliver for them. Not surprisingly, they want to attach themselves to leaders they see enhancing their own performance. Resources play an integral part in these calculations. In fact, questions about a leader's ability to lead frequently coalesce around resources. They provide an early indicator of the power and influence the newcomer can bring to bear.

When Cathy Benko was asked by the CEO to take over the Women's Initiative (WIN) at Deloitte, to say she was reluctant is an understatement. She was not at all sure the firm still needed such a program, nor was she sure she was the one to lead it. But through the extensive research she did in collaboration with leaders in the firm, she became convinced the program could still add value and started to see herself as the person to lead it. She knew, however, that to revive the Initiative, she would need to symbolically reposition it.

Her negotiation had two parts. The first was to secure WIN a seat on the executive council. After all, if it was a strategic initiative for the firm, it should be treated as one. Second, and just as important, she needed the CEO's commitment to give WIN the budget it required. It had been underresourced for several years, and she knew that to have any hope of repositioning WIN in the firm and the marketplace, she needed a real commitment—so she negotiated hard for it.[1]

If you ignore the symbolic dimension implicit in resource allocations, you leave yourself open to continuing doubts about the organization's commitment to the job you are taking on. Soon those questions spill over and begin to color perceptions of your ability to act on your agenda or to lead at all. While all leaders in new positions are tested, the scrutiny can be especially intense for women. They are often under the microscope with people waiting to see how they fare. That close inspection makes the symbolic statement behind resources all the more important. It signals to colleagues and subordinates alike the value key stakeholders put on the effort you are undertaking. It also goes a long way in resolving any uncertainty about your ability to deliver.

COMMON TRAPS

Many women take on demanding assignments only to find, as Old Mother Hubbard did, that the cupboard is bare. Additional resources are hard to come by in organizations today. At a recent conference for woman leaders, for example, we asked the group how many had been mandated to fix a problem or implement significant changes. Almost all hands shot up. We then posed a follow-up question: How many had to take on these tasks without additional resources? Over 80 percent answered in the affirmative. Collectively the women faced the prospect of doing more with less.

The scenario captured by that vote is the rule these days rather than the exception. Limits on resources create tough choices. In obvious ways they make hard jobs harder. But in one significant way they simplify matters. Priorities, always imperative, take on even greater urgency. Yet two traps distort the decision-making process and encourage new leaders to bypass prioritizing altogether. Keenly focused on budget constraints, they assume that they can cope and set out to fill the resource gap by acts of will. Alternatively, conscious of every dollar spent, they can fail to realize that certain expenditures have a hidden impact—on visibility or morale that far outweighs the outlay. In both situations, what looks like careful husbanding of resources gets no credit from other leaders and is criticized by those directly affected.

- "I can pick up the slack."

It makes practical sense for anyone taking on a new assignment to figure out how to do more with less. But that process has political implications as well, particularly when it postpones any real resolution. A temporary remedy—*I'll make do and keep productivity up with what I've got*—can put the unwary in an unsustainable bind. Expectations never get adjusted to the resources available and poor results are traced to a lack of effort. Alternatively, even when you produce the desired results through sheer determination and grit, the work behind them goes unrecognized and so expectations of more resources go unrealized.

Margaret was caught in this bind when she was tapped to launch her firm's latest line of products in a new market. In taking the assignment, Margaret knew she would need funds to support the marketing effort. She would also have to draw on the capital of various people within the firm. Not only could she use their expertise; their standing within the community would ease her transition. Preliminary conversations with her new boss were encouraging, but they produced no definitive commitments. "He told me that he would see what he could do," she says. Excited about the prospect, Margaret figured that she would get what she needed once she was in place and could demonstrate some results.

Margaret threw herself into the work, making the connections she needed and picking up the slack when others in the firm did not immediately come forward. She found herself "working long hours at a killing pace."

> I didn't spend a lot of money to get this done. From time to time I did ask for additional resources. I did need help from other people. But neither the resources nor the help ever materialized.

Margaret's requests were denied in part because her own actions showed that she was getting along fine without them. She was doing all the work herself, without involving others in the firm and with limited resources. No one had any reason to think that she would not continue to deliver. In particular, she gave her boss no incentive to divert resources her way. But the consequences went further. Margaret got the launch off to a good start by working day and night. When it came time to choose a leader for the emerging market, Margaret was passed over. The consensus was that she was a good worker but did not have what it took to be a leader.

- "I have to keep costs under control at all costs."

New to a position, it is only logical to concentrate on bringing a project in on cost or meeting a budget. That may be one of the reasons you were selected in the first place. The trap here is not efficient management of resources. The problem comes when it becomes an end in itself.

People in the organization watch resource allocations carefully, looking for important clues to the backing you enjoy.[2] But the real test of resources often comes from members of your own team. In many organizations, people make choices about leaders they want to work for and with. *Will you have the influence to secure the resources needed to do our work? Are you the kind of leader who will use what you have to motivate your team? If I join your team, will the decision benefit my career?* These questions are all subjective, and perceptions shape the answers. At this level, resources are not line items on a budget, they are symbols of influence.

The symbolic nature of resources eluded Sally when she took over as head of global technology services for an international firm. Promoted over her peers, Sally had to battle the perception that she did not have much influence with leadership. These hidden doubts came out into the open over an off-site meeting where top leadership planned to launch its new corporate initiative. With cost cutting rampant throughout the company, Sally decided that her budget would not support increases in travel allowances. She gave the go-ahead for group members to attend the meeting—provided, however, that they did not run up any airline or hotel costs. As is often the case today in corporations, Sally's team was spread out over many geographical areas. This decision effectively put an end to the group's participation in the meeting and her team complained (more to each other than to her). Sally dismissed the complaints as sour grapes; these people, she concluded, didn't recognize how important the corporate mandate to control costs was.

While that may have been true, Sally too was shortsighted. The travel costs were relatively modest compared to the opportunity. Top leadership was kicking off its most important strategic initiative in years and her people attended only by satellite hookup. Key members of the group concluded that she really did not have any influence with key leaders in her division. If she could not wangle the dollars for them to go to such an important meeting, she certainly would not have the clout to garner the resources for the ambitious plans she had laid out.

STRATEGIC MOVES

In today's world, it is not easy to attract the resources you need. One of the women we interviewed talked about having "a senior brief without the checkbook." Funds for new initiatives may be difficult to secure. Getting people you depend upon to give you their time and effort, their human resources, can be especially challenging. Four strategic moves can help as you negotiate these resource issues.

- *Align requests to strategic objectives:* Resources are symbolic blueprints. They outline where an organization is and where it intends to go. The closer you link your agenda to those strategic objectives, the easier it is to make the case for the resources you need.

- *Appeal to the interests of other stakeholders:* There are often other stakeholders to your agenda even if they are not obvious. Their ability to produce results may depend on yours. These overlapping concerns create interdependence. Because your appeals mesh with their concerns, these stakeholders can often be persuaded to bring indirect influence to bear on the allocation decision.

- *Enlist allies to support the case:* People have multiple motives to support a request for resources. Maybe they benefit directly. Maybe they like to be associated with innovation and new initiatives. They may be able to make a case for what you need better than you can do yourself.
- *Leverage success:* There are many potentially creative ways to secure resources. Pilot projects, segmenting parts, and working things out over time can produce small wins that can attract additional resources

Donna Fernandes employed these strategic moves to marshal the resources needed to rehabilitate the Buffalo Zoo.* In this chapter, we follow her progress as she makes her vision for the zoo a reality.

Donna brought a doctorate in zoology, an MBA, and ten years' experience working at other zoos to the Buffalo Metropolitan Zoo when she was selected as its CEO and president.

> *I had worked for a year for a design firm that had done quality master planning for clients around the world so I understood what a good zoo could look like.*

She would need all those credentials and experience. The Buffalo Zoo did not begin to approach her vision of what a zoo could be. It had last been renovated during the Roosevelt administration, a beneficiary of its public works projects. The third oldest zoo in the country, the Buffalo Zoo also had an outdated infrastructure. Donna's predecessor, in fact, wanted to scrap the existing plant and move to a new site.

> *My predecessor thought that there was so much wrong with the place, let's start fresh. He spent three years spinning his wheels, dreaming this incredible, unrealistic dream of building an eighty-acre zoo right at the waterfront. The cost was astronomical—$160 million. All of that money had to be raised at once because you cannot open a new zoo with one exhibit.*

Note: In earlier chapters we have disguised the identities of the women whose stories we tell. We make an exception for Donna Fernandes because her resource campaign is so rooted in the Buffalo community.

> The lack of reality behind this ambitious plan forced the board into action. They brought in Donna to rehabilitate the zoo. To do that she needed a plan—a vision for the zoo and a strategy for getting the resources to realize that vision.

Align Requests to Strategic Objectives

To secure the resources you need, you have to show the benefits to the organization. People must see the connection between your needs and broader objectives. The lion's share of resources goes to people who take care of critical contingencies for an organization.[3] In the university world, for example, many departments depend on outside grants to fund research and defray a portion of their overhead. As a result, the ability to secure research grants has become a core competency with prestige attached to it. In a complex intersection, prominent researchers attract internal resources because they have demonstrated their contribution—measured in actual dollars—to the department or institute's continuing financial viability.

Strategic objectives vary over time and within organizations. They may address a critical problem or capitalize on an opportunity. Whether an initiative focuses on problem or opportunity, however, its claim on resources correlates directly to its likely contribution to the organization's broader objectives and well-being. Attracting the right people is critical to any rapidly growing organization and thus executives who recruit and hire usually have priority claims on resources. By contrast, in a down economy, those go to the people who manage costs. The closer you can tie your resource requests to critical objectives, the greater your chances of having your proposals heard and requests met.

Demonstrate That the Resources You Seek Will Solve a Big Problem
When people perceive threats to their environment or envision significant opportunities, they are more open to appeals for resources that will help the organization deal with challenge. Good issue sellers—people who are able to influence change from the middle—know that it is easier to get their message across if they connect it to strategic threats or opportunities.[4]

Hannah highlighted both the threats and the opportunities when she was appointed to a new leadership role in her financial services firm. "Our business model was under pressure," she says. "We needed to think outside the box and create the business of the future." The current structure—"the way roles and responsibilities were delegated"—was not producing results. Nor was it likely to help the organization adapt to future demands. There had to be more senior-level accountability, sponsorship, and thought leadership.

Hannah faced countervailing pressures that could squeeze needed resources away from this future-oriented project. "We still had to deliver current results in a world of limited resources." Structural changes take time to implement. Their impact on the organization and the bottom line does not show up immediately.

> This trade-off between short-term results and the commitment to a longer-term vision can be very hard for line people to make. Deliverables in the future don't have the same visibility or predictability. No matter how important the work is for the organization's future, it can get lost.

Hannah built her case for committing resources to the redesign by carefully balancing an analysis of where the firm was against the vision of where it needed to go. Short-term results could not be produced indefinitely at the expense of long-term change. Both were equally important to the organization's health. If, however, no changes were made, current productivity would not pick up.

> People have short-term attention spans. You have to be very clear and help them connect the dots. You have to remind them why you are talking about this issue. Why it's important to the future. Now we are at A or B. Draw the correlation. What will it take to get to C or D?

The changes envisioned would not only increase accountability, they would create greater transparency and adaptability—making it possible for the organization to become more nimble and take advantage of opportunities to grow its market share. The explicit connection

Hannah made between resources and future possibilities secured her the resources she needed.

Whether you are dealing with new systems or new organizational structures or a problem area that needs to be turned around, the link to strategic objectives supplies a critical rationale for diverting scarce resources to the effort. Connecting what you need to what is good for the organization makes asking for the resources you need feel more defensible and be less likely to invite backlash.

Connect Resources to Likely Outcomes

Demonstrating the potential value of an initiative can be a challenge. Yet if people cannot see the value, they may be reluctant to make the resource commitment. In framing the value proposition, you need to consider your audience. How are various people likely to view your promises and your requests? Individuals respond to different stimuli. Some are drawn to compelling initiatives. Others look for clear financial explanations.

Pilar, the new vice president of development for a major cancer research institution, knew that meeting the board's ambitious goals required significant investment. The development office was under-staffed and its technology antiquated. The board had agreed on the goals. Now Pilar had to convince them to commit the necessary resources to the effort.

To build credence for the numbers, Pilar conducted an internal audit. She used the data to develop a detailed plan "several inches thick, right down to development office's space needs over the next three years." She also included a one-page summary.

> The plan was so thick and so detailed I knew the trustees would only read the summary. That's where I wanted their focus.

The president arranged for Pilar to present the plan to the four most influential (and vocal) trustees. "These were businesspeople on the board, not the doctors. They appreciated the executive summary that connected the funding we were asking for to revenues." The summary called for investment in resources—hardware, software, space, bodies—but promised to deliver $60 million in new funds within three years. The incremental costs were only $10 million—a huge jump in the fundraising world. "It's sometimes easier," Pilar says, "to get something through that is bold, something people can get excited about, rather than nickel and diming and predicting a 5 percent or 10 percent annual increase."

The benefits did not escape the notice of the four trustees. They threw their weight behind the plan and soon the rest of the board signed on. The decision paid off. Pilar's office raised $80 million by the time the three-year deadline was up, and it had a staff of 110. But the resource challenge remains ongoing. Fundraising targets increase each year and strain the supporting infrastructure—particularly the information technology systems. With hospital resources hard-pressed just to meet the needs of patient care, Pilar says, any request from fundraising has to be justified by a predictable and ample outcome.

The connection of input and output cannot be just a rhetorical device to build a convincing argument. You do not want to be trapped in a commitment to a project that is not viable given current constraints. Certain minimum thresholds in resources need to be correlated to the results possible. For example, when Connie took over the leadership of a major sales effort, she made the connection between resources and outcome explicit to the executive committee. "Yes, I will do this," she explained. "But I cannot do it for $2 million. That is like throwing $2 million out the window." In part, Connie underscored the minimum funding threshold because she had a reputation for delivering. She had to make the executive committee understand that nobody, not even she, could produce the desired results without adequate resources. It was better not to undertake the project than to carry the twin burdens of unrealistic funding and high expectations.

Align Resources with the Ebb and Flow of the Work
The resource demands on any organization are not static. They fluctuate with the seasonal sales cycle. External events can bring certain strategic

issues to prominence while others ebb in importance. Being responsive to this ebb and flow demonstrates that you are in sync with the strategic needs of the organization at different times. Recognizing where a project is in the business cycle, for example, can make it easier to secure resources when they are needed.

Alison, a biotech executive, has to be especially attuned to timing and its impact in resolving the conflicting demands on limited resources. Alison leads several cross-functional teams that take a drug from the time its chemical formula is discovered through the FDA approval process. Even with an annual budget upwards of $40 million, Alison finds it challenging to ensure that the drugs she has under development move steadily toward FDA approval. Working within a matrixed organization, she must compete with other team leaders for human resources—the various disciplines that bear on any drug trial.

"Once we get approval, we can start marketing and making money." As a result, projects that are closest to market have the highest priority when it comes to resources. Alison uses this decision rule in bidding for resources. She might, for example, justify pulling a cardiologist off another team leader's project if that expertise were needed to meet a critical submission date on one of her projects. When Alison's projects slip behind on the schedule, she evaluates the implications and then decides whether or not to raise the issue.

> We have to make trade-offs—the major one being time for people. I only make waves when I really need to. In a crisis, we can go outside and hire expertise. But I weigh that decision carefully before putting in the request. It's expensive to go outside and that decision has to be justified by the costs of the delay.

Alison's approach—linking resource requests to stages in the development process—frames demands in terms that the head of R&D understands. Because some delays can be costly, he listens when she flags a potential problem and points out the probable ramifications if additional resources are not allocated. In making the case, understanding the pressures and claims the other person is up against helps. That way you can tailor your appeal in a way that shows you understand their situation.

> After the rebuff of the previous CEO's plans, Donna Fernandes knew she needed to make the strategic case in order to garner sufficient resources to rehabilitate the zoo. First she needed a vision.
>
> *You are really selling a dream. You need a vision, a plan, that is exciting and compelling and unified.*
>
> Donna rejected the usual solutions.
>
> *I don't like zoos without any rhyme or reason behind their organization. Some just separate taxonomic groups. This animal class or that one. Others concentrate on bio-geographic differences. This is South American; this is African.*
>
> Donna wanted a single story line that would tie all the exhibits together. She found it in water.
>
> *Water really defines habitats—desert, grassland—and the patterns. Water is also a relevant story for this community. A hundred years ago, Buffalo was a center for transportation with the Erie Canal. With Niagara Falls we were the first city to have hydroelectric power and electrified streets.*
>
> Donna developed a plan that wove together different stories of water. It included a South American rain forest with a dramatic two-story waterfall; an Asian river system; and an African plain with a big watering hole where animals congregate. She also included an arctic exhibit focusing on frozen water—snow.
>
> *People loved the plan because it told a logical story of how water influences life on the planet, and the Great Lakes are the country's largest bodies of fresh water.*
>
> However appealing the organizing water theme, Donna still needed to show that her vision would make a significant difference to the zoo's visibility and revenues. But first she had to respond to the zoo's immediate needs. Her predecessor, in efforts to build support for moving the zoo, had emphasized that the existing plant was not worth saving. "People were talking about how old everything was; how decayed everything was."
>
> The zoo was also about to lose its accreditation. The dilapidated building housing the primates and big cats did not meet the standards of the American

Zoo and Aquarium Association. Fortunately, Donna had $2 million in county funds, appropriated when the zoo decided not to move, that she could tap. She used that money to seed the rehabilitation of the main building.

> *We designed the exhibits to feature threatened or endangered species. I was trying to reposition us and called the exhibits "Vanishing Animals." We had an interactive section about how scientists study endangered species, what habitats are at risk. Everything that we did was about repositioning the zoo—we breed endangered species, we are involved with leading programs.*

The rehabilitation saved the zoo's accreditation, obviously a key issue for her board. It also ended up costing $4 million. Donna was able to raise the difference as people began to see her vision take shape. By dealing with key strategic issues, Donna secured the initial resources to launch the zoo's transformation.

Before Donna began the resource campaign, however, she was completely candid with the board about the range of possibilities. She explicitly linked what could be accomplished to the resources they could garner. Her message to the board was blunt.

> *For $20 million I could give the zoo a facelift. We would keep what we had, but improve the visitors' experience and the lives of the animals. Or we could spend $70 or $80 million and completely refurbish the zoo, creating an educationally enriching experience with really cool exhibits. If you don't think we can raise $80 million, then let's not kid ourselves. There is no point in having one wonderful corner while the rest remains mediocre.*

Donna carefully aligned the decision with her vision of what the zoo could become, but she was equally emphatic about the need for realism.

Appeal to the Interests of Other Stakeholders

It helps to align requests for resources to an organization's strategic interests. But individuals base decisions on more than strategic needs and problems. Their personal interests matter as well. If you want people to say yes to committing resources, they need to see that the decision will help them too. In other words, appeals need to be relevant to where people are. This resonance is especially important when it comes to human resources. (In fact, good people may be the most important resource of all.) Before people are willing to get behind an agenda, they have to be convinced that it resonates with their personal needs. There are several ways to illuminate the congruity of interests.

Focus on Key Interests
We tend to assume that people have only a limited number of interests and restrict our appeals to those. Unfortunately, financial incentives may be out of the question given budget constraints. Opportunities for promotion may be narrow. If, however, you go beyond the obvious and learn something about people's real interests, you may find other concerns that count with them.

Amanda, for example, discovered that interactions with professional peers mattered to her team members. When Amanda was promoted over several colleagues to head a research department, questions about her selection surfaced. To quell them and learn more about the department, she went to work to find out what her team members needed. She discovered major inequalities between her department and a parallel one doing similar research. Despite the parity in work, the scientists and engineers on Amanda's team considered the other department more prestigious. It got better computers and enjoyed more generous travel allowances. Each was a sore spot for people who prized both virtual and actual interactions with their peers.

> I knew I needed to equalize these discrepancies. My appointment had been competitive and unless I could deliver for my team it would continue to be questioned. So I went right away and advocated for equivalent resources.

Amanda's boss, who had several department heads reporting to him, was unaware of the friction or its causes until she pointed them out. Amanda knew her boss had multiple interests. As much as he wanted to keep costs down, he also wanted to be fair and to keep morale—and productivity—high. She used the last two to negotiate with him over the disparity in computer upgrades and travel allowances.

> I showed him places where we could make adjustments in the division's overall budget in order to meet my department's needs for travel and

equipment. The increase in my budget was modest, but it enabled me to
show my people that I had advocated for them successfully.

Amanda's probing for specific needs turned up a collective interest
within her department. By emphasizing the congruence with her boss's
interests, she paved the way for a negotiation that benefited both her
boss and her team.

Structure for Early Warnings

In most organizations, people have multiple responsibilities that force
them to make trade-offs when deciding how to spend their time and
their energy. If your request for resources helps them plan and eases
this pressure, they will be more likely to make the commitment.

Elizabeth, a director of contract research, constantly competed for
scarce human resources. Her company, with $1.6 billion in sales and
sixteen thousand employees, provided contract research to pharmaceutical companies. Requests for proposals (RFPs) came in all the time.
When they did, Elizabeth had to "pull people away from their day jobs"
to work on proposals. These proposals, although not revenue producing,
were the key to the company's future revenue stream. Elizabeth, in fact,
was evaluated on how many RFPs "hit"—produced research business.

Before Elizabeth took over as director any RFP triggered a crisis.
People would scurry to put teams together in order to get a response
out the door. To counteract this crisis mentality, Elizabeth created an
early warning system between sales and operations.

> Any RFP requires input from various functions and from the research
> people. We carved out a floating team and built in a layer of expertise.
> Therapeutic expertise—say, psychiatry or oncology—had to be coupled
> with operational expertise. Previously key people might not have been
> available. But with a ten-day average lead time on proposals, we could
> anticipate those needs and anyone could plug into the process.

The rationalization of the process had several benefits. It allowed
people across the company to anticipate demands on manpower and

to prioritize among the various RFPs. It also ensured that people with client contact would be involved in crafting responses to RFPs, making tailored proposals more likely. Moreover, Elizabeth instituted weekly meetings where she could update key leaders on anticipated needs. They in turn used these updates to anticipate demands on their own resources.

Make Differential Appeals

Not everybody's interests are the same. Time matters most to some people; others value visibility. Understanding these different motivations can help a leader leverage modest resources into a broader commitment.

When Maggie took over as executive director of a battered women's shelter in western Massachusetts, the agency was floundering. The precarious financial picture, if not improved, would force curtailment of its strong direct services programs.

> The bottom had fallen out. The way things were structured with federal and state funding it was difficult to downsize. A lot of staff positions were funded through specific grants. They covered salary, but not general overhead or administrative costs. If I eliminated that position, I lost that funding and those services for, say, $3,000 in overhead savings. That position might also be connected to another service that gave us support or legitimacy.

With public funding drying up, Maggie turned to her New York fundraising background for inspiration. "I had to marshal a whole new level of resources to keep the programs afloat."

> In New York City people want their names in lights—as bright as they can get for however much money they give you. I started working with celebrities. I would describe how women and their kids arrive here—with nothing. I asked them for donations—personal stuff, whatever. But the best thing you can give us would be your ideas. Design a room that you would feel comfortable in, a room where you would feel safe, coming from a traumatic situation. I got Gloria Steinem to design a room. I wrote a letter to Maya Angelou. She loved the idea. In fact, she ended up doing a pro bono benefit.

But Maggie also looked to the community, pondering how she could approach people who did not want to be that visible.

> We launched a campaign locally—"Be Part of the Solution." It went to where people were—to what they had to contribute. We enlisted vets who sheltered animals when families were trying to leave bad situations. We recruited trained hairdressers who got an earful while they were doing a shampoo and blow dry. We persuaded mechanics to donate time to fix a car.

To get people to commit time and resources, you have to make it easy for them to say yes. That means tailoring appeals so that they fit the individual or the group.

Donna Fernandes had multiple stakeholders when she embarked on transforming the Buffalo Zoo. The county executive and the legislature controlled the public purse. Buffalo's citizenry was vocal and concerned. Prominent members of the community could influence public opinion and kick off efforts to raise private funds. Each group had different interests. And Donna realized that each would respond to different aspects of her vision for the zoo.

> *The community groups were up in arms. The previous director, planning to move the zoo to the waterfront, never articulated what would happen to the vacant site. There were fears that it would become a major target for vandalism. His predecessor had been willing to keep the zoo in its original location, but proposed taking over the park. So all the joggers, golfers, and tennis players would have had to go.*

The Buffalo Zoo is located in a historical park designed by Frederick Law Olmsted. Donna went to the historical commission and got a strong letter of support for her plan.

> *The zoo's current footprint is Beaux Arts and very linear, formal, but stockade fencing blocks the view to the park. The whole design of the new project is very much in the spirit of Olmsted. It restores the vistas and uses water. The Olmsted Conservancy loves the plan.*

Donna took that endorsement to the community and support began to build. She delivered a quite different message to the county executive and the legislature. An investment in the zoo would reach large numbers of their constituents. The zoo had the widest demographic of any cultural institution in the Buffalo area.

Despite the zoo's condition it still attracted more than twice as many visitors as the Museum of Science. The Albright-Knox Art Gallery, an outstanding museum housing contemporary art, appealed to a narrow segment of the population.

Donna commissioned visitor studies to dig deeper into the comparative data.

I discovered that the zoo's visitors had the greatest range in educational level—from preschoolers to Ph.D.'s. We also had a great range in income level—from poverty level to wealthy. There was great diversity in ethnic backgrounds among our visitors. All those statistics documented the zoo's appeal. It was not just a question of numbers but of range. A lot of people feel that the Albright-Knox is beyond them. You can know everything there is about animals and still love the zoo. Or you can be a total Bozo and still love the zoo.

Donna realized that visitors equal voters. "I kept pounding that point with the county executive, with the legislators. In giving us $8 million, they would be investing in an institution that benefited their constituents."

Donna's major private donor concentrated on the business plan. Donna peeled it back layer by layer, all the time relating it to her vision. Her targeted approach paid off as she built a coalition to secure the resources she needed.

Enlist Partners to Support the Case

In today's organizations, competition for scarce resources can be intense. Any case grows stronger when its support comes from different quarters. In fact, in certain circumstances, you may not be positioned to make the case alone. Maybe you have presented similar requests so many times in the past that people who can commit the resources no longer listen attentively. Maybe, despite your formal position, people do not feel that they have to take your entreaties seriously. Or maybe the request requires such a heavy commitment that it needs a broader show of solidarity. This is where allies and partners come in.

If you think about the various stakeholders in an organization, you can map them across a spectrum. There are people you work closely with and trust. These are your allies. Then there are others, as discussed in Chapter One, who block your efforts. In between these two poles lie potential partners. These are what Herminia Ibarra has called *allies of convenience* or *bedfellows*.[5] They may be willing to join with you in certain circumstances—when their interests align with yours. And because they bring different perspectives and sometimes represent different functions, they can help build a sharper, more comprehensive, and more persuasive argument.

Enlist People with a Stake in the Decision

Certain people are natural partners of convenience. They have a stake in the resources you secure because the allocation benefits them as well. Lorraine enlisted just such a partner. Lorraine's strategic consulting firm had just come off a series of layoffs and its top leadership was reluctant to fully staff an engagement before revenues started coming in from the client. "It's a Catch-22," Lorraine says. "For a time, until you get ramped up, you are underdelivering."

Matters came to a head for Lorraine, whose role was to develop business, when a new client, a major one, was unwilling to sign a contract without evidence that the firm had the dedicated personnel to fulfill it. "My objective was to accelerate the hiring and to shift people around internally." The contract would generate sizable revenues over an extended period, and Lorraine did not want to jeopardize the business because it looked like her firm lacked staff to do the work.

Lorraine's firm has a matrix organization structure. Aside from business development people like Lorraine, it has relationship managers who have client P&L responsibility and capability managers who oversee billability. "Our goals were very different," Lorraine says. "The capability manager liked the potential revenue the client would bring in, but he wanted to manage the process so that we were highly billable and profitable, net/net, at the end of the day."

She took her relationship manager to visit the client. "I hoped that once he understood that they were really concerned about the staffing, he would be willing to hire ahead of the curve. We needed to hire consultants who would be 25 percent billable starting out and then ramp them up." Lorraine worked with the relationship manager to sell that idea. Lorraine, as the business developer, could not argue the case to the capability manager as persuasively as the relationship manager could. He could credibly demonstrate the potential in that particular client relationship and bring greater objectivity to the discussions—or at least the perception of greater objectivity. Lorraine got the resources she wanted and the client is now a major contributor to the firm's revenue stream.

Enlist People with Specific Expertise

Certain people can bolster your case by supplying specific expertise. A specialist, say, in channel marketing lends credibility to any request for funding to support an expansion in distribution. The head of R&D can speak to the design of a research project. A leader in the organization's IT department can verify the need for backup data storage systems and corroborate the costs in dollars and time. When partners like these get behind a request, they give that request greater depth. They add substance to the argument. But beyond contributing specificity, their knowledge base commands attention. They know what they are talking about, and this credibility then attaches to your request.

Jackie, an expert in sales training, revamped the programs at her company by partnering with the executive vice president of finance. Having a Ph.D. in education, Jackie knew she would need a partner to present a credible financial argument for her initiative.

Jackie took over training for the residential real-estate group of one of the nation's largest banks during its annual budget process. The bank aimed to become the country's number-one direct provider of residential mortgages. But the situation in the field was changing rapidly. Loan originators needed to locate potential clients through real estate agents, financial planners, and attorneys; they could no longer rely on leads from the branches. Conversations with the line quickly told Jackie that training was not doing enough to support the loan originators.

With the annual budget still in process, funding levels had not been fixed. Jackie estimated it would take at least $3 million to meet the needs of the five thousand originators in the field. To make her case, she collaborated with an executive vice president of finance. Together they used a Six Sigma process to do a deep dive on the business case. After that dive, he was convinced. Not only would the investment pay off, it was essential—underfunding would jeopardize *any* return. He had no hesitation in supporting the $3 million threshold when it came up for discussion during the next meeting of the executive committee.

That support was key for Jackie. When it came to budget decisions, committee members found it easier to accept the judgment of someone from finance than the assertions of a specialist in training.

Enlist People Close to the Situation

People closest to a situation often know the most about it. They may be able to capture the ramifications of impending allocations for decision makers who are somewhat removed from day-to-day operations. This local view brought an added dimension to Terri's ongoing negotiations over resources.

Over the past two years, Terri's consumer products company had cut its professional staff by 25 percent. Of course, there was no comparable reduction in the workload. Terri, the director of an R&D group in the food division, needed to align resources with capacity. She started by convening meetings that brought together key decision makers with members of her group to set priorities. "We were being run ragged by demands from product development," she says. "This guy wanted a study on cakes; that one wanted to test another flavor in the bottled water. On and on."

At first people complained about what they dubbed "Terri's Priority Sessions." But the meetings turned out to be great. Her staff members would come in with their priorities. The senior leadership in Market Research and R&D did not have to do any work; they just had to show up. As the staff ranked projects, the senior people were always surprised at how much work Terri's department was doing.

These presentations made the department's work visible and underscored the trade-offs between capacity and resources. The meetings also forced decisions, but the people doing the work now influenced those decisions. There were times when Terri would seed the meeting so a particular person would make a particular case.[6] Terri worried about losing her effectiveness as an advocate if she was always advocating. "It helps," she says, "to enlist others to do it with you."

> Donna Fernandes enlisted partners, sometimes on a contract basis, wherever she could to bolster her resource case. She used experts to sell her big plan to foundations.
>
> > *We hired master plan consultants who laid out all the new areas, provided sketches of the habitats, and estimated prices for construction. They also estimated new staff that would have to be hired and developed projections for attendance and revenues. The whole business plan along with the master plan was something that foundations wanted to have. It was a complete plan, rather than a couple of bubble diagrams.*
>
> Once the local historical commission became convinced that the zoo would preserve the integrity of Olmsted's original design, its members became full partners. Their approval ameliorated community worries. Not surprisingly, Donna drafted her board to help make the case with influential members of the community. But she went out of her way to involve everyone:
>
> > *Every time someone comes up to me and thanks me, I tell them, "Why don't you call the county executive or the legislators and thank them."*

Leverage Successes

Resources are not always secured in a one-shot, all-or-nothing deal struck around budget time or when you are first appointed. Often they are the result of a staged campaign. No matter how creatively you negotiate, when you are new to a role the risk is perceived to be high. Prudence may caution decision makers to hold back and see what you can accomplish with the resources in place.

You can sometimes get over this accomplishment hurdle by delivering a contained and modest demonstration project. By design, pilots or demonstration projects put less strain on resources. They also attract scant attention if they do not work out, yet when they are successful, they produce *small wins* that can be leveraged.[7] Their narrow scope restricts both the new leader's exposure and the organization's. Yet the small wins they generate can supply the evidence you need to make a credible case for additional investment.

Once a successful demonstration project becomes visible and you are credited with the small win, you can go after bigger hits.

Bite Off a Small Piece of a Big Pie

When an ambitious initiative with a big price tag is introduced, support can be equivocal. Ambivalence should be expected. Big efforts usually bring big risks. Yet ambitious plans can often be broken down into smaller, incremental pieces. These smaller bites can be rolled out quickly and with a minimal drain on resources. With each success, the quest for additional funding becomes easier.

Katlyn, a department head, started small when she was trying to change the way her team did business. She was convinced that if they were more proactive, there was a strong possibility that her group could convert the service calls they received into sales opportunities. Katlyn carefully considered how to build the case for the very expensive sales infrastructure that would be required. A realist, she presented the idea to her boss, requesting that only one more person be assigned to her team as an analyst to calculate the amount of additional revenue that could be generated. Because the added expense was modest compared to the potential profit, he agreed. It didn't take Katlyn long to summarize the data in support of the transformation.

Pilot a New Idea

Resistance to a project's very concept can make securing funds for it difficult. A pilot project, a small version of a big idea, can elude the notice of potential critics. Alternatively, they might not pay much attention and raise no real objections to a small investment. But once launched and successful, the pilot gives you persuasive evidence justifying further expansion. Carrie, for example, introduced an ambitious effort to attract business from women entrepreneurs with a small pilot project.

The bank had been tossing around the idea of setting up a unit targeting women. They had been making loans, but there was no cross-selling of services or investment products.

Although Carrie's estimate of the potential market exceeded $100 million, she asked for modest funding to do a pilot. This bare-bones request was intentional. The scope of the project allowed Carrie to "fly under the corporate radar" during a critical testing period. "I didn't step on any lenders' toes or get in the way of the account executives"—at least not then. Carrie fully intended to roll out a multistate program. The successful pilot not only vindicated the plan, it also gave her a platform from which she could talk about funding that larger project.

Small wins like Carrie's pilot can also build institutional momentum behind an initiative. And because success breeds success, these small wins can generate big hits in the future. With each incremental gain in support and visibility, it becomes easier to attract resources. A mathematically minded technology executive reduced the observation to a formula:

> If you get 5 percent of the organization on board, they can influence the next 15 percent, and then you can bring the organization over the hump. Once you get to 20 percent, the organization can move.

Build on Tangible Results

In trying to secure needed resources, the when can be as important as the how or the what. Sometimes no amount of stretching can get you what you need. The wise approach may be to work for visible, sustainable results and use them to make the case. Simone, a division vice president of operations, secured additional resources for her overworked department, but not without increasing their workload temporarily.

At the time of Simone's appointment, the division was already underfunded. Part of a larger conglomerate, the group supplied a full range of services for corporate events, including transportation. Recently, however, revenues plummeted and the parent company mandated a series of layoffs. As a result, Simone faced a serious dilemma. She needed to get rid of poor performers, but to make her revenue goals she also had to bring in new people who could do the work.

Simone realized that she could not make a case for bringing in new staff in an uncertain environment where people were being laid off and revenues had dropped precipitously. Instead, she went after a major client. "No one thought we would get the company to sign up," she says. Then she targeted another key account. These two clients alone represented more than $1 million in profits. The additional business looked good on the bottom line, but it stretched the department to the limit.

> People were working intense hours. These new accounts could tip them over the edge. The department would collapse if we continued that way.

Simone's success in the marketplace demonstrated that the division could succeed. The CEO of the parent company could see, with the two new accounts, indications of a marked improvement in the division's business environment. To serve these accounts and grow the business, however, Simone needed to hire additional people. The CEO gladly underwrote the next million. Simone's new accounts alone had netted the division that much in one year.

Donna Fernandes attributes her success in garnering the resources to transform the Buffalo Zoo, in part, to her ability to build constituencies. She managed to assemble all of these with small wins, one step at a time.

- The $2 million in county funds she used to start rehabilitation on the main building preserved the zoo's accreditation. The visible project generated sufficient interest that private donors stepped up and filled the gap, providing the other $2 million needed.
- Dialogue with the historical commission became a full-fledged partnership.
- The (not so) small win of the main building renovation convinced the board to back the more ambitious plan of a complete refurbishing rather than take the safer and less costly route of a facelift.

Donna remembers what people thought about the zoo when she took over:

When I first came here, I would get e-mail: "I just brought my family to the zoo and I was appalled. How can you keep those animals in those ugly cages? You should be ashamed of yourself."

With a vision and a strategic plan, Donna gathered the resources required for the zoo's transformation, step by step. As a footnote to her story, a columnist from the *Buffalo News* visited the zoo with his two daughters. A week later he interviewed Donna. Then he wrote a column headlined "Leadership Conquers All at the Buffalo Zoo."[8]

❖

Resources determine, to a large extent, what you can accomplish in a new assignment. But their impact is felt on two distinct levels: First is the practical, where trade-offs must be made between capacity and investment, between inputs and outcomes. But resources also carry symbolic weight. They are prime indicators of what an organization thinks important and who can be trusted to exercise judgment and leadership.

It is essential that women—whose influence and credibility can be questioned—pay acute attention to the resource issue. Good people want to work for good people, and resources are a tip-off to many of just how good someone is.

GET READY TO GARNER RESOURCES: STRATEGIZING TO NEGOTIATE KEY ALLOCATIONS

Resources are needed just to get the job done. But wishing and hoping won't make the right allocation magically appear.

It is dangerous to assume that you can make do with whatever is offered. You risk burning yourself and your team out. You train others to expect you to go along with allocation decisions without protest. And, most important, you lose credibility with those you lead.

Align Requests to Strategic Objectives
Building a business case for the resources you seek is not optional. You need to be clear about the resources you will need, both immediately

and for the long term. Before people sign off on allocations, they must be convinced that the investment will pay off.

- Does your resource case link the request to a business imperative? Do people see the connection?
- What is the likely return on investment of the resources you seek? How long will it take to see results?
- Have you correlated specific resource levels to the results that can be achieved?
- What can you tell people about your likely resource requirements for the future? Do you anticipate that your needs will shrink or expand? Under what circumstances?

Appeal to the Interests of Other Stakeholders

You are not the only one who will be affected by the resource allocations you negotiate. Look for other stakeholders who will feel the impact. When their interests align with yours, it is not hard to persuade them to support your case.

- Who would be hurt if your allocation falls short? How does your work help them to meet their goals and objectives?
- What motivates the people you need to convince? How can you appeal to their interests?
- Can you make the allocation process more efficient? Are there ways, for example, to build in early warning systems so that people know when and where resources will be needed?

Enlist Partners to Support the Case

You can never have too much help or too many people backing your request for resources. You can strengthen your case by calling on partners with specific expertise or specific needs.

- Where does your business case need shoring up?
- Who might have the expertise to validate your request or the credibility to vouch for your needs? An in-house expert? A customer?
- What would it take to persuade them to help you make that case?

Leverage Successes

Quick hits—small projects that do not drain resources—can produce big results when they are leveraged.

- Can you establish the merits of a larger program by launching a pilot?
- Are there any elements of your agenda that can be isolated to produce quick results?
- What projects can be used as test cases?
- What outcome would everyone consider a "home run"? What metrics are or need to be in place to measure the results?

CHAPTER 4

BRING PEOPLE ON BOARD

Negotiating Buy-In

As Adam and Eve left the Garden of Eden, he took her hand and said, "We are about to enter a time of transition." Leaders today face a similar prospect. No matter how good their intelligence, how strong their backing, and ample their resources, they are venturing into uncharted territory. If our interviews are a good indication, leadership appointments of the routine sort are relics of the past. Not a single woman we interviewed took on a new assignment expecting to be a caretaker. Instead, the women confronted roles that demanded they shepherd change. Some were called upon to revive flagging departments or whole enterprises. Others, in the wake of mergers, faced the challenge of marrying disparate cultures. Still others sought to get new initiatives off the ground—either bringing new products to market or introducing new internal systems.

The risks of leading change are great. That's why Ryan and Haslam label these assignments when given to women as the "glass cliff"—it's easy to go over the edge.[1] Any change affects people as individuals, as members of a department or group, and as part of an organized system with accustomed habits, personal ties, and culture. Any change breeds support from some, resistance from others. Yet the old guidelines of what it takes to be a leader no longer provide much guidance—or comfort.

In the face of rapid technological progress and intense competitive pressures, the new leaders we interviewed were thrown into situations where they constantly had to reinvent themselves and their roles as leaders.

It is not that change automatically breeds resistance. But when change brings with it the possibility of loss—threatening comfortable ways of doing things or long-standing loyalties—it can precipitate formidable resistance. Because that resistance often focuses on the new leader, it can be characterized as a personal vendetta, undertaken for parochial or shortsighted reasons.[2] It may well be. But just as new leaders must constantly adapt to fluid circumstances, they must encourage their peers and subordinates to adapt as well.

To get peers and subordinates to put their weight behind a change agenda, you must first convince them that you can lead them through it successfully. You have to engage them on your agenda. They need to know that however threatening departures from past practices might appear at first blush, there is something to gain from them. You cannot impose change, as in the older hierarchical organizational models. Rosabeth Moss Kanter captures this new reality: "[As] the clear distinctions of title, task, department, even corporations blur, traditional sources of power erode and the old motivational tools lose their magic."[3] You have to bring those involved to the understanding that the opportunities of the new outweigh the costs of giving up some of the old. You are, after all, asking them to step outside their comfort zones. They have to start to trust you.

Some in the business press, in fact, often give the edge to women on this front. Socialized to care about others, the reasoning goes, women early on develop an aptitude for collaboration and hone their ability to connect with others. They supposedly have a greater tolerance for ambiguity, appreciate the efforts of teams, and, accustomed to juggling multiple roles, exhibit greater flexibility than their male counterparts do. These skills and inclinations should stand them in good stead when they need to enlist buy-in from their team. .

Unfortunately those relational abilities that mark the "feminine" style—the ability to mentor and to foster collaboration and open dialogue—do not necessarily work to the advantage of women. Doubts about their abilities, causing them to feel they are under a microscope to perform, may force them to adopt exacting standards. And those standards can in themselves breed resistance because, as discussed in the Introduction, a woman who expects a lot can be criticized for not being feminine enough. This is more likely to happen in certain male-dominated environments and when there are few women in leadership roles.[4]

If, however, a woman taking on a new role emphasizes the feminine side of leadership—the nurturing, supportive aspects—she is likely to be considered too nice. Relational skills, long associated with a woman's predilection for nurturing, may not add to perceptions of her leadership ability. They can be discounted as traditional women's work. Her male colleague, on the other hand, gets kudos for the courage to show his softer side and for his attentiveness to the concerns of others.[5]

To convert a change agenda into a shared agenda, women must often navigate in this uneasy territory between what is expected of a leader and what is expected of a woman.[6] That can be an uncomfortable place from which to bring people on board. The challenge is to help peers and subordinates deal with their very real (and quite legitimate) fears and to move past that initial resistance. A key to getting peers and subordinates to pay attention is for the new leader to pay attention. Most people don't resist change because they take pleasure in being obstructionist. They can back up their objections with what they consider valid reasons. They may even think that the change effort is pointless.

Women leaders in new positions face dual challenges: They must establish commitment to the task at hand and develop a communal commitment at the same time. On both counts, they can anticipate resistance and must have strategies in place to overcome it. The objective is to convince these potential naysayers that change is not only possible but, with their help, likely.

That objective makes for a delicate balancing act. The leader needs to bring her team on board by creating a context for them to contribute and by enlisting them to work with her. To do that, she must rely heavily on relational skills—responding to her team members' concerns and appreciating the difficulties they have experienced in the past and those that they see ahead. But she must couple these connected overtures with moves that establish her credibility as a leader.

Because connection is so closely associated with women, it is important for women leaders to work on both levels: simultaneously establishing their own decision-making authority and engaging others in the decision-making process. Before team members sign on, they must be individually convinced that you can make those choices, that you won't back down at the first hint of opposition or resistance, but that you will appreciate their concerns and find ways to deal with them.[7]

COMMON TRAPS

Women taking on new leadership assignments risk springing traps in two ways. Because their natural leadership ability may be questioned, they can try to impose it without earning the authority first. Perhaps they overcompensate and want to appear strong from the start or perhaps they consider their mandate sufficient grounds. Team members resent the imposed solutions and their resistance grows. Alternatively, recognizing that they do not have implicit authority, women new to leadership emphasize consensus and fail to set concrete expectations or provide direction. To subordinates, who have concerns about change to begin with, an undiluted communal approach can be unsettling. They question the new leader's ability to lead them through the changes. Neither approach gives team members any incentive to get on board and back the new leader's agenda. Here are four common traps in negotiating buy-in that we isolated from our interviews.

- "I know what I'm doing is the right thing to do."

Few take on a new role without having some specific ideas about how it should be played. They glean these notions from past experiences or from watching others in similar roles. Nor do new leaders want anyone to think that they are unprepared and have not thought enough about the problem. So they come to the assignment armed with an action plan that frames not only what they want to accomplish but how they are going to go about it.

Thoughtful preparation does not spring the trap. That preparatory work is vital. The trouble arises when the new leader becomes so enamored of her plan that she cannot hear what others are saying. *There is nothing wrong with my plan,* she thinks. *If people resist or disagree, I must not be communicating effectively. I haven't been persuasive enough.* So she starts to persuade—and the one she persuades most is herself. The disagreement is treated as a failure of communication, and in a certain way it is. The communication is going only one direction.

It is not unusual in any disagreement for people to think that the basic problem is one of communication. *If only I can explain things clearly,* they think, *the others will agree.* Unfortunately, many objections are not the result of miscommunication. The other parties simply do not agree and can substantiate their differences of opinion with solid reasons.

The risks of attributing disagreement to faulty communication are twofold. First, chances are slim to none that people can be persuaded to get behind an agenda they consider misguided, overly ambitious, or insufficient. Second, because their concerns or doubts have not been heeded, their resistance is likely to be greater.

Denise, a marketing executive at a manufacturing company, had been with her firm a long time. When she was recruited internally to handle procurement, a problematic area, she brought a full-fledged strategy with her.

> The company was in trouble. Although I was new to procurement, it was clear to me that they needed someone to take a strong stand with the vendors. I quickly put into place a new set of cost-control systems. Procurement would become a policeman in curtailing costs.

Denise made a series of presentations to senior management and the people in her group. Professional and clear, they showed the logic behind her approach. Procurement, however, had relationships with vendors and with department heads throughout the company that went back twenty years. Denise's team members had maintained those relationships and wanted a solution that tempered what clearly needed to be done with the realities of their day-to-day interactions. They saw themselves as service providers who negotiated good deals with vendors and already talked department heads out of unnecessary purchases. Denise threatened that collegial atmosphere. She found that it was easier to call for a policing function than to make it a reality. More experienced than she, department members found ways around her policies. Discouraged, she resigned.

Denise had a big strike against her when she took over as head of the department. She was new to procurement. Establishing her credibility was going to be a challenge, but she exacerbated the situation by assuming she could change the systems. She assumed she knew best and that the department members would come around if only she were persuasive enough.

When real differences exist about a change agenda, attempts to impose the agenda simply send the resistance underground. Buy-in evolves only if the differences are allowed to surface and are confronted.

• "This is really my problem. I have to work through it to protect my people."

Sometimes leaders internalize the problems they inherit. They feel responsible for *solving* those problems. Wanting to make things better, they try to shield others from difficulties and take care of them. Thinking of the problems as *their* problems, they hold them close. They fail to solicit other opinions or ask for help. Not only does this approach keep team members in the dark, it cuts off avenues for possible resolution. It can alienate people who want to help, and it can also take a physical and mental toll on the leader.

Three weeks after Sylvia took the reins of a new initiative at her bank, it was acquired by a much larger institution with a national footprint.

All our planning for the new initiative was suddenly in jeopardy. Everyone was preoccupied with the merger. Nobody wanted to know about
our plans.

The new parent had always grown by acquisition. After a spate of
mergers it had little practice in organic growth or the customer-oriented
program development that had characterized Sylvia's organization.
Sylvia put on a bright front and kept these headaches to herself. Little
by little, the nascent trust within the new team began to wane. They
had heard the rumors. They knew the parent's reputation for not
valuing people and cutting right to the bottom line. What they did not
understand was Sylvia's reluctance to engage them so that they could,
together, develop a convincing sales pitch for the initiative.

Sylvia thought that the bad news would demoralize members of her
team; she wanted to protect them. The situation was quite the opposite.
They would have welcomed the chance to participate in working out a
way to keep the initiative alive until a decision was reached. Instead, they
interpreted Sylvia's silence as an ominous signal. When she finally had
a chance to meet with the parent's head of new business development,
she got a green light for the initiative. But by then the damage had been
done; she had lost some of her team and had to work hard with those
remaining before the project could be mainstreamed.

- "I have the support of senior management; people will fall
into line."

Backing from top management can get new leaders and their
agendas off to a strong start. But that is what it is—a strong start. The
strength of their mandate can lull them into complaisance or they can
exaggerate either the level of support or its impact on their team. If they
have been overly optimistic in judging the strength of their backing,
they can get caught off guard when that backing disappears with the
first sign of a problem. Alternatively, what they consider a strong plus
can turn out to be a liability if their team thinks top management does

not grasp the realities in the field. Claire, a regional executive recruited to lead a large sales force, found out the hard way that a mandate from the top was no guarantee that her team would embrace her agenda.

> Coming from another company in the industry, all I could see was opportunity. The company had a strong, established brand; nationwide market trends seemed to be great; yet the region I was recruited to manage had not been making its sales targets. Top management recruited me aggressively and pretty much gave me free rein to shape things up. That's what I tried to do.

What Claire did not know was that the sales force had been working hard and had accomplished as much as they could in a difficult economy. Managers and salespeople alike were convinced that top leadership was completely out of touch with the local market. They had been hit hard by the cuts in the manufacturing sector. When Claire raised their quotas despite deteriorating market conditions, they saw her as just as out of touch as top management. At every opportunity, they ignored her and her decisions and continued to conduct business as usual. Their reaction influenced the CEO. While he didn't know much about the market, he looked at the numbers carefully. When he saw no improvement in the region, Claire's mandate evaporated.

For team members to get behind a new leader's agenda, they have to make a judgment that fits with their sense of the situation. By itself, a strong mandate from the top may not be sufficient to convince them. They require some proof that their new leader's agenda can add to their effectiveness and is not simply imposed from above.

• "Avoidance is my best short-run strategy; best to just give it time."

New to a position and on unsure territory, it is tempting to think that things will work out with time. Eventually, fence-sitters will see the advantages of the new agenda and get behind it. Eventually, even the resistant will be convinced. It is better to let things settle down before attempting to do much.

Avoidance does not make the difficulties disappear. In fact, time can favor those who hold out. The longer you delay in confronting resisters—whether the opposition is overt or covert—the more likely it becomes that others will coalesce around them and threaten to block your agenda.

When Tricia, a tax partner in a national accounting firm, was promoted to managing partner for the western district, she took on responsibility for top-line services in the marketplace. Tricia knew when she accepted the promotion that she would have issues with certain partners in the district. She was also venturing into a different part of the business. She had never before had responsibility for generating revenues or developing new business opportunities. Meanwhile, Bill (one of the district partners), had extensive experience and had actively campaigned for the promotion. Tricia worried about him at first, but he welcomed her warmly. She assumed she would have time to get their relationship on an even keel. If that failed, she could always ask the regional partner to reassign him. Tricia's first hint of real trouble came with her plans for a retreat.

> The partners in the district all acted as independent agents. They were a freewheeling group. To meet my growth targets, that culture had to change. As soon as I arrived, I scheduled a retreat for the group. That would be an opportunity to get to know one another and for us to develop a coordinated strategy for the district.

People were excited about the retreat. It would be a first for the district and give them a chance to do strategic planning as a group. The day before the retreat, however, Tricia got a voice mail from Bill. He could not attend. He had an important meeting with a client. Tricia was furious, but decided not to make an issue of his defection.

Tricia expected that her efforts to build team cohesion would gather momentum after the retreat. Instead, they stalled. She started to have problems getting information from two of the other senior partners. Bill took credit for new business she brought in. Conversations broke off suddenly when she came into a room. Associates began to go to Bill for approval.

> I didn't know what to do. If I confronted him, he would get defensive. If I was too accommodating, he would continue to undermine me.

Once resistance solidifies into open opposition you have two choices. Avoidance is not an option. You can try to neutralize the resisters by raising the costs of continued obstruction, or you can see if you can get them assigned elsewhere. Allowed to remain in place, they can influence the rest of the group and stall any effort to build cohesion. Not only does unwillingness to confront resisters signal weakness, it gives the rest of your team cause to doubt your ability to make other hard choices.

STRATEGIC MOVES

One of the women we interviewed likened taking on a new assignment to filling a leadership vacuum. That characterization may fit from the new leader's perspective, but it probably misses the mark when it comes to the people who will end up reporting to her. There's no void where they are concerned. They have long memories. They know what worked in the past. Most have looked long and hard at what the appointment might mean for their careers or their daily routines at work. Maybe some of them thought the job should have been theirs.

Recollections of a predecessor are particularly fresh, both on the positive and negative. Whether team members rate their previous boss as middling or superb, it can be a tough act to follow. Happy with the way things were, they just want things to continue as usual. On the other hand, people may be happy to see the other person go and look forward to you taking over. But at other times, the situation prior to your arrival may have been so bad that the team is demoralized and holds out little hope that the situation can be retrieved.

Your reception is clear—whether they welcome you or not. But you need your peers and team on board. How do you energize the resigned and the doubtful so that they work with you? What can you do to give the fence-sitters a push? And what do you do with the stubborn resisters after their probation period runs out? Four strategic moves can help you unify a team behind an agenda.

- *Go on a listening tour:* In the interdependent world of business today, few leaders elect to go it alone or issue orders by fiat. By listening closely to your team members, by being actively curious, you can discover their hopes as well as their fears. By listening closely to peers across the organization, you can draw out their perspectives. Attentive listening shows them that their opinions matter to you and can have value for the organization.
- *Help solve problems:* As the team waits to see what you will do, you can build support early on by understanding what their critical issues are. To the degree that you can solve some of their problems, they are more likely to join with you on a broader agenda.
- *Forge broad links:* Your peers stand in particular relationship with you. Some will have real stakes in seeing your agenda succeed. They stand to gain if it moves forward or lose if it stalls. Alliances forged across the organization not only propel the agenda forward, they make team members feel less isolated. By forging these links, you can create momentum behind an agenda and so isolate those peers who would rather see you fail.
- *Create opportunities to learn:* Change challenges adaptability. By expanding people's capabilities, finding where they can be successful, and giving them the tools, you enable them not only to adapt to the new realities but to flourish there.

Buy-in depends on recognizing interdependencies—linkages in work, in accountability, in rewards, in concerns and interests between you as a leader and your team. The connection that produces buy-in is not a superficial smoothing of discord or compliant peacemaking. It requires appreciative work to listen hard, work to respond to concerns creatively, and still keep everyone on track.[8] It requires work and not a little fortitude to make hard choices.

> Linda Green faced hard choices when she was recruited to be president of Clarendon Capital, a small Portland investment bank wholly owned by a large financial institution. She also took on the assignment with several liabilities. A banker with more than twenty-two years' tenure at BankOregon, she had been running specialized lending—automotive, restaurants, and telecoms. She was what in the trade is called a "relationship banker." The portfolio at Clarendon Capital, however, was a mix of mid-market debt, buyout equity, and venture capital investments, and Linda knew virtually nothing about the venture side of the business.
>
> Moreover, Clarendon Capital was in trouble. It had suffered significant losses in its venture and funds portfolios, and the IT and telecom investments were overleveraged. Linda did not want to be a "substitute teacher," cleaning up the balance sheet only to have someone else come in.
>
> Linda did, however, know the chairman and vice chairman of the parent from her days at BankOregon.
>
> She respected them as people and as businessmen—an important factor in her decision to accept the offer. "There had been," Linda says with measured understatement, "a dilution of credibility in terms of key managers at Clarendon Capital."
>
> Although the Clarendon Capital group was small, it was divided into fiefdoms. Junior people felt "isolated in their silos, at the whim of personalities." The senior people had lost the board's confidence. No one was certain how long the doors would remain open.
>
> Linda had to get the financial house in order. But she aimed to do more than rescue Clarendon Capital and reduce the risk level of its portfolios. Linda wanted to grow the company. Her people were the crucial determinant in whether that would happen. As she described her first year on the job—the focus was people, people, people.

In this chapter, we follow the strategic moves she makes to energize the group and bring people on board.

Go on a Listening Tour

It is pretty standard these days for new leaders to start their tenure with "listening tours." As one of the women put it at a recent conference: "You need to show up and listen." Teams expect it of a leader and of a woman. But listening tours are not just another item on a new leader's checklist—a task that can be performed in perfunctory fashion and then crossed off. Listening tours are a time to get acquainted—to find out what is on people's minds and to let them know what is on yours. Secretary of State Hillary Clinton's first overseas trip designed to begin to repair the image of the United States abroad was described as a "global listening tour."[9] It was the same approach she used in the state of New York when she ran for the U.S. Senate, visiting scores of rural communities around the state to learn about their issues. She made a point of saying that she believes strongly that "we learn from listening to one another."

Listening tours encourage participation. Attentive, responsive listening goes a long way toward convincing people that you are curious about them and their situation. They convey that you want them to do well and will help them adapt to the new realities. They begin to see points where the new agenda may align with their interests. But they won't get that far—either with you or with your agenda—if they sense that they are being manipulated. Nor will they bother to participate if the gesture comes across as a shallow attempt to conform to organizational niceties. "Making nice" is not a surrogate for connection, although it is often mistaken for one. A leading executive coach advises the "intimidating" women sent to her by their companies for counseling to "listen up until you want to throw up."[10] This advice denigrates the listening process and belittles the acuity of the very people that her clients want to engage.

Find Out What's on People's Minds

Most listening tours begin with one-on-one meetings with the key members in a team or unit. Just as you want a positive introduction

when you take on a new role, subordinates want an opportunity
to introduce themselves and get some of their issues on the table.
Typically these individual meetings cover a range of topics that touch
on the personal as well as the professional. One leader described her
approach:

> I asked three questions: First, tell me about you? Anything. Work, family,
> whatever. Second, what do you do here and how is it working? Third,
> what are you hoping for—two years out, three years out, in ten years?

These one-on-one meetings are an occasion to get to know your
people in multiple dimensions. They also help you understand the major
issues in the group and begin a process of collaborative problem solving.
Listening, with genuine curiosity, you can take the group's collective
pulse.

Cynthia, an engineer with an MBA, took over as vice president
of engineering at a technology start-up when the current COO was
promoted. Despite Cynthia's engineering background and experience,
earning the respect and cooperation of the technical people was a
challenge.

Cynthia's company supplied sophisticated Internet security systems.
The firm had survived most of the fallout when the economy faltered,
but Cynthia detected uneasiness in the labs and in the offices. "I met
with every single person in the unit. I wanted to find out their concerns
for the company and for themselves. I wanted to know what was
worrying them." The technology slowdown was an obvious source of
concern.

> The individual engineers, the technical folks, felt marginalized, that their
> skills were unappreciated. Many of the teams felt marginalized as well.
> Partly these feelings reflected a residue left by my predecessor. He was
> abrupt and made decisions by fiat and so the engineers felt that they
> had no say in their jobs. I listened to them with an eye to restructuring
> job assignments in ways that would make them feel that their skills were
> being used and make the entire enterprise more productive.

But Cynthia also found out that her staff had other concerns. As billable people in a volatile market, they were worried about that next project. Cynthia knew that she needed to find ways to remove this source of anxiety if she could. It was one of the first concerns she addressed.

In taking time to figure out what is on people's minds, you uncover information that enables you to shape your agenda, making some issues priorities and letting others wait for resolution. Dealing early on with what is on people's minds, not only do you signal your concern, you also make it more likely that you will be able to produce some small wins that mean a lot.

Take the Group Pulse

However important it is to find out what is on people's minds, these issues and concerns may be quite parochial. That does not mean they don't matter, but a listening tour also needs to uncover more about the business issues a new leader has been called in to work on. While there may be consistency across a set of individual stories, just listening to individuals may focus you too narrowly.

Taking the group pulse inevitably pushes the new leader to engage different team members in a group activity, be it a series of small, informal meetings or an off-site retreat. These events serve multiple purposes. They become places where concerns can be shared and debated. An interesting phenomenon can occur during this process. As people tell their stories and listen to others, they often come to see the situation in new ways. The new leader can build on that experience and help fashion an agenda that members can buy into. That is what Kate did when she took over an R&D support unit for a consumer products division after her company merged with another.

After meeting one-on-one with the seventy-five scientists and a large administrative staff, Kate organized an off-site retreat. With the help of a facilitator, Kate summarized for the group what she had learned from her one-on-one conversations.

The group confronted two major issues at the retreat. First, they wanted to craft a shared mission. Since the group was the product of the recent merger, finding an identity was critical. In the group session, members talked about being buffeted by the demands that other departments put on them. Working together, they came up with a team slogan—Bringing Senses to the Table. This motto defined their work as providing product insights. Two aspects of Kate's approach were pivotal in enabling the group to reach this common place. She shared what she had discovered in her one-on-one interviews and then orchestrated a process that made it possible for individuals to talk about their concerns about the newly merged organization.

The second issue the group faced was gaining a sense of themselves as a unit and not as two competitive factions artificially thrown together by a merger. Each person in the group had taken a style assessment and that exploration of their differences was built into the retreat's structure. "We could talk about our style differences and remark to one another that it was great that there was so much diversity in the group," Kate says. But it was through the process itself—which put the group to work on its issues—that they came to appreciate the strength of their diversity.

Exchanges like these provide a peculiar kind of safety net. They cut down on the uncertainty and ambiguity that arise whenever someone new takes over. In sharing ideas, both the benefits and the support implicit in the new agenda can become clearer.

Listen Outward

A listening tour would be limited indeed were a new leader to stop short and not seek out assessments of her group from other quarters of the organization. It is standard practice for a new leader to meet with external customers and clients in order to get a fix on the systemic problems that need to be addressed. But any group also has internal clients that command attention. Unless you listen to them as well, you cannot understand how your group is viewed within the organization at large. You also risk overlooking significant points of interdependence.

The nature of the organization you lead determines whom you consult and how critical that consultation is. For Eleanor, internal consultation was essential to her mandate when she was put in charge of information technology for a consortium of health care plans. Top management saw health insurance moving toward consumer-directed plans, and good systems were the cornerstone of the firm's ability to serve consumers individually rather than through an employer.

Eleanor initiated a series of meetings with key stakeholders—her peers in other departments who used the services IT provided. These included vice presidents in sales and marketing and health care services.

> They told me that we talk in a language that nobody outside IT under-
> stands. We overcomplicate things. We're not very responsive—especially
> to complaints when a system goes down or they're having trouble with
> some new software.

From inside IT things looked radically different.

> The team was frustrated. They felt that nobody listened to them or appre-
> ciated the work they accomplished under considerable constraints. They
> had processes that they had inherited that didn't make any sense. People
> complained, but team members didn't feel empowered to suggest fixing
> anything.

The change agenda carved out a central role for IT as an enabling tool. Before Eleanor started talking to people, she worried about buy-in internally within IT. Her subsequent explorations told her that she would also need buy-in from her peers—the consumers of IT's services—to address the problems at the operational level.

Complex problems generally have complex sources. Attempts to fix them spill over in multiple directions. The more you know about those spillover effects, the better able you will be to anticipate them.

It is telling that Linda Green started at Clarendon Capital on December 17. Most people do not start new jobs on December 17. But Clarendon was regulated by the Federal Reserve, and the Fed audit was scheduled for January 29. "It was quite clear," Linda says, "that the sooner I got in the better."

Many in the parent company were old BankOregon hands, and they welcomed Linda. They would say: "Oh, we knew you from before." "You have a great reputation." "This is a great place to work." The atmosphere within her group, however, was tense. It was generally acknowledged that the time was ripe for "the people who got them into this mess to leave. The jobs of three and possibly four of the senior people were on the line."

Even with the holidays and the Fed audit, Linda spent an hour and a half with each person in the group.

They were afraid. I wanted them to see that I had two interests at heart: their success and the unit's success. It was not hard for me to show them that we could align those interests so that we could create value between the two. I did this by helping them envision their futures in a revitalized investment bank. I told them that I was fully prepared to give them new responsibilities—and would help them learn—as we restored the bank's health and started growing again. Developing their skills was good for their careers and good for the bank.

By being open and transparent, Linda used these discussions to emphasize the change of regime. "The transition was going to be tough," she says. Management procedures needed to be improved, guidelines established, and underwriting criteria tightened. "The agenda would put an enormous administrative burden on everyone."

Previously the senior people controlled individual fiefdoms. There was no cohesion as a group, no sense that the various functions were interdependent. Linda did not sugarcoat the work ahead. "Time out," she would say.

All hands on deck. We have a lot of things to do. And we need people to jump in on an as-needed basis. If four financings are up for renewal or need add-ons, and all four belong to one person, everyone must help.

If members of the group saw a sudden expansion of their responsibilities, they also did not miss the benefits. Whereas earlier they might have been cordoned off in mid-market finance, now they would have opportunities to get involved in venture investments or leveraged buyouts.

They felt good about that. Instead of thinking only about how they were doing, they started to think about how the group was doing. There was

*much more camaraderie. We were going in a new direction. We were not
going to look back, but forward.*

As Linda got acquainted with her team, she carefully balanced twin goals:
she wanted her people to shine as individuals, to be successful in what they did,
and she wanted to make Clarendon Capital the thriving enterprise she believed it
could be. She saw no dichotomy between the two, but rather synergy.

Help Solve Problems

As you listen and make connections, you gather information and shape
perceptions of you as a leader and of your agenda. The responsive,
appreciative inquiry that characterizes effective listening tours creates
an atmosphere in which team members can begin to consider the
possibilities ahead for them. Nothing immobilizes people faster than
uncertainty. Anxiety can be tempered by listening attentively to concerns
and sharing expectations and plans. It will not, however, disappear.

Talk is not enough. Actions need to be taken. People have to
see that you are doing the things that promise change for the better.
Obviously, you need to start correcting the issues you were brought in
to address—and are committed to resolving. If you move too slowly,
you raise questions about your competence. Moving too quickly and
exercising a heavy hand, however, can be equally risky. It is a fine line.

In the early stages of a new assignment, you want to create the
conditions that make it possible for those you lead to work effectively and
move the new agenda forward. Those conditions may involve individuals
and their deployment—ensuring that the right people are in the right
jobs. These may need to be created at the group level—implementing
enabling structures so that the group becomes more productive. Or
they may have to be introduced at a systemic level to remove barriers
to high-level performance.

Fix Individual Problems

Practical considerations focus a new leader's immediate attention on
staff matters. Not only do you want to get things moving, you want to

show people right off that you are committed to helping them be more satisfied in their jobs and more productive in their work. During listening tours, new leaders find out about individual interests, preferences, skills, and experience. They can put those discoveries to good use by aligning assignments more closely to individual objectives while at the same time deploying team members in ways that benefit the entire organization. Cynthia, the Internet security firm vice president we mentioned earlier, took what she learned and began to address the concerns she heard expressed about uneven deployment. Based on individual interests, she restructured some jobs.

> I respected their career plans—who wanted to move into which areas. I tried to get to know them as individuals and position them so that they had greater job satisfaction. This shift led to some increased efficiencies. Dealing with the unpredictability of the work, however, was more difficult.

Demand for engineering services could be erratic. Sometimes people were overloaded, but at other times they had little to do. Under pressure to cut costs, Cynthia could have downsized the engineering group and used contract workers to cope with the ebb and flow of the workload. But Cynthia regarded that option as a last resort. The economy would turn around soon, she believed, and she wanted to keep her highly talented pool of engineers engaged and involved. The challenge was to find ways to use the engineers that created value.

Cynthia knew from her interviews with key stakeholders that potential internal demand for the engineers' expertise existed elsewhere in the organization. Departments like procurement had been waiting a long time to upgrade their systems.

> I would invite—not assign—people to take on certain projects that would benefit other groups in the company. They could turn them down if they wanted to. So the product groups began to see us as a resource that could help them. The engineers also began to feel that I was looking out for their interests. They were busy and they were adding new applications to their résumés.

When a new leader solves problems at the individual level, she signals that people's interests and concerns are being credited and acted on. Although it is possible to think about fixing individual problems narrowly and consider only the impact the solutions have on individuals, the women leaders we interviewed did not frame their approach that way. Certainly they were willing to coach and spend time with their people. But in dealing with individual problems they looked for synergistic solutions that worked to the benefit of the organization as well as the individual.

Address Group Problems

Group problems are those that interfere with the group's productivity. Addressing these issues can mean removing barriers that hamper performance. Rules or procedures may no longer fit the realities of how the group does its work. The group may need greater insulation from outside interference so that its members can focus and not be continually distracted.[11]

Margot, newly appointed director for one of her company's software products, knew she would need to take action to salvage her team and its product. When she took on the role, due to cutbacks during the slowdown in technology sales, the unit's staff was overworked. As a result, they were not meeting delivery deadlines and customers were complaining that the product had too many bugs. Margot knew that if they did not deal with the quality control issue, there was no way she could get the unit back on track. She assigned a test team to dig deep into the problems the group was having. She wanted to know exactly where they originated in the production sequence.

The test team's report was illuminating. The breakdown was not in programming or production. It was in a poorly written user's manual and lack of support that confused customers. Prior to her arrival, her team had already spent over nine hundred hours dealing with the wrong problem. By quickly addressing the group problem, Margot freed up her team's time and enabled them to begin work on the software's next release.

Sometimes, a group problem has more to do with morale and a sense of defeat than with a faulty system or procedure. Leah was recruited from the California State University system to help a Midwest college get its physical therapy program through accreditation. The appointment carried a deanship, but by and large the faculty were skeptical. Having been turned down before by the accreditation board, they were convinced they could not succeed.

Leah tried to show them ways that they could succeed, that it was possible. She brought in course syllabi from other institutions and across a wide range of programs. Leah knew the faculty's materials suffered by comparison, but she wanted to provide a model for them to emulate. With Leah's encouragement, the faculty began to talk about the weaknesses in their materials and how they could develop a curriculum that would meet the accreditation criteria. This positive attitude spread into other program areas, and within a short period the program had passed its first milestone with the accreditation agency.

Addressing group problems means creating the structural and psychological conditions for the group to do its work most productively.

Engage Systemic Problems

In identifying and dealing with group problems, your focus remains on the group's internal workings—with those issues that individuals or the group as a whole single out as concerns. Systemic challenges, by contrast, you discover through interactions with people outside your group—the other stakeholders who have been part of your listening tour. Engaging systemic issues can be a major undertaking, requiring a thorough cultural assessment and reorientation. But systemic problems can also be addressed more modestly through incremental changes. It is this modest course that Eleanor, the head of IT in the health care field, pursued once she discovered the negative light in which key stakeholders viewed the IT department.

Eleanor recognized that IT's internal clients did not value the work her group was doing. In turn, their constant complaints frustrated her group. Eleanor knew that she had to break this cycle if she was going to turn things around. At an off-site meeting, she relayed to her group what she had learned from key stakeholders on her listening tour. There was, they decided, a disconnect between the group and its major internal customers. Relationships were not being managed well. Working with her senior team, Eleanor realigned job responsibilities to create project managers. These managers would be the primary interface between IT and its users. Collectively, the group agreed to streamline forms and communicate more clearly and in ways the clients could understand. Eleanor also appointed a small group to investigate which technologies were too cumbersome for users.

> The group really appreciated what we did. At last, they could see some progress. First, I appealed to their prime frustrations and tried to alleviate those. But beyond that we focused on how we could add value to the organization by tying IT's services back to the critical things the organization was doing.

Tackle the Difficult Problems

When you're new to a role, you have many choices for how to proceed. One alternative, which can also be a trap, is to wait and see how things play out. But a problem can be so pressing that a new leader's credibility rides on dealing with it immediately. Often that problem is someone who is not performing. Making determinations about performance can be tricky. Is the person coachable or not? But in other cases there is no debate. Everybody is aware of the problem, even if they keep their opinions to themselves. The situation is like the proverbial elephant in the room that people see but do not mention. Taking on the elephant's organizational equivalent can be a critical moment in the process of creating buy-in. That is what Beverly faced when she became CFO of a venture capital firm.

When Beverly interviewed for the job, people told her about the controller. Then during her listening tour she discovered just how chaotic the accounting function was. Reports were late and filled with errors. "His office," Beverly recalls, "was a cave, filled with papers, piles and piles of faxes and spreadsheets—a controller who was clearly out of control." The clutter was symptomatic of the general, disorganized malaise affecting the whole finance function.

Having identified the problem, Beverly also knew she needed to tread carefully. The culture was one that valued loyalty. People were not likely to look favorably on a peremptory firing as her first act. But Beverly also knew she had to act. At first, she tried to work with the controller.

> I started to push. In the beginning we met once a week, then three times a week and then twice a day. The more the controller withheld information, the harder I pushed. One day after a particularly difficult meeting, he resigned. This pattern had a history. He had resigned three times before and the partners had begged him to return. The controller was surprised when I accepted his resignation. Everyone else was relieved.

The practical benefits of confronting difficult problems early are obvious. Less apparent is the symbolic value. However hard it may be to deal with a poor performer, for example, the decision sends a pointed message: You can make the tough choices needed to maintain morale and move everyone forward. For a woman, moments that call for decisive action can be pivotal. Others watch and wait. Unless—and until—you move to resolve difficult issues, these observers will continue to question your ability to take charge.

> Linda Green underscored her commitment to champion not only the group but also its individual members by going to bat for one of the people top management had slated for termination. After talking with him, she decided the decision would be a mistake. Linda noticed that he was not a good advocate for himself. He needed someone to repair the damage that was accruing to him from the three other senior executives who were culpable. She sat down with him so they could figure out what to do.
>
> > *Look, here's what might have happened; here's why it didn't. But there are things that we—you and I—need to do together to change the perceptions of [top management]. They don't have confidence in you right now. He was very, very happy that I was honest with him.*

That connecting move brought the unit together. Linda had no Machiavel-
lian intent. She thought it was the right thing to do. But in standing up for this man
and not going along with top management's initial recommendation, she gave
the members of her group concrete evidence that she saw them as individuals and valued what they could contribute. Moreover, Linda left no room for her
responsiveness to be interpreted as weakness. She let two other senior people
go, although the separations were amicable.

Forge Broad Links

Your team and direct reports are not the only ones whose buy-
in you need. The objectives of peers across the organization may be
intertwined with your agenda. When you enlist these peers as allies,
you build momentum behind your efforts. The quotient of positive
energy increases with each additional level of support. People notice the
growing consensus.

Winning coalitions require strategic and political thought to assemble. But their impact on a team can be pronounced. They provide
psychological reassurance and a critical safety net for your group. Subordinates quickly realize that they are not hanging out there all alone
with you.

Offer Help

The quickest, and often the surest, way to get support from peers is to
show that the changes you are implementing will make their lives easier.
And the simplest way to demonstrate that improvement is by offering
help—letting them experience firsthand the effects of the changes. Even
natural competitors think twice about blocking efforts that add to their
bottom line and make them look good with customers and bosses alike.
As others in the organization notice the benefits, you can bring them on
board as well.[12]

Stacy was tapped to head up a newly formed unit at her financial
services firm. Her handpicked team was all on board. Resistance from
other sectors, however, was pronounced. The unit, a response to the

chairman's emphasis on "relationship marketing," targeted the firm's top seventy clients worldwide. It was no surprise to Stacy that its creation sparked turf battles. "People in sales considered, say, Janus their property. But Janus also happened to be one of our top seventy accounts."

Rather than accept the inevitability of the conflict and fight with sales over a client, Stacy decided to help them. Their end objectives were the same, serving the firm's clients and growing the business.

> My teams did a lot of research on our clients. This was research that sales couldn't or just didn't do. We analyzed our clients' strategies, competitive positions, and cultures. Sales would claim they knew the key decision makers, for example. But often their information or sources were just plain wrong or not senior enough.

Stacy did not hoard this information to gain a competitive edge on sales. She shared it. Within a short time key people in sales began to depend on the analysis that Stacy's group provided. She no longer had to "twist arms" to be included in strategic planning meetings, and her team felt appreciated rather than beleaguered. News of the success spread by word of mouth around the company. Members of Stacy's group were ecstatic. They had, after all, managed to be in the right place at the right time.

Resistance to a change agenda springs not just from within but outside. Other groups within the organization can view the contemplated changes as threats to their objectives. Offers to help go a long way toward dispelling these fears. When the help actually makes people's lives easier and furthers their mission, resistance can abruptly dissipate. Former blockers become surprising allies.

Enlist Help

Change agendas are difficult to implement alone. They often cut across functional disciplines. Even when new leaders recognize the complexity and interconnectedness of the task, they can resist seeking help. They view it as a sign of weakness. That reasoning is based on a faulty premise.

You are asking people to work *with* you, not to come up with solutions *for* you. Once others are engaged, they can bring different perspectives and resources to bear. And as they become involved, they begin to own the problem with you and to have a stake in its resolution.

Laura, a consultant whose clients included major players in the health care and pharmaceutical industries, was drafted by the CEO of a premier biotech firm to head its business development wing. "In biotech, business development is synonymous with mergers and acquisitions or divestitures," she says. One operational unit caught her immediate attention. It was small but losing money rapidly. The CEO wanted to keep the division; everyone else wanted to sell it outright and get rid of the problem. The CEO asked Laura to draft a strategic plan. He liked what he saw and promptly appointed her division president so that she could implement the plan. "That is every former consultant's nightmare—having to execute," Laura observes wryly.

Laura's plan called for selling three of the division's businesses and closing one plant. An outright divestiture would have been easier. The company had never had a layoff. Everyone on the inside doubted Laura's plan could succeed. The economies of scale argued against it.

Laura appealed to the head of human resources for help. Loyalty was an integral part of the company's culture and a big selling point in attracting talent. They could not let the plant closing and the layoffs undermine those bonds. Laura also turned to the chief financial officer. The plan projected marked productivity gains. Some of those cost savings could be anticipated and applied to relieve laid-off workers. The chief financial officer created room in the budget for transition costs. The head of human resources worked with Laura to make the closing seamless. As a result of their help, Laura was able to offer displaced workers placement services and generous separation benefits. "Sixty of the sixty-six employees found comparable work in a month or so," Laura says.

The level of cooperation Laura mustered in support of the division impressed her remaining employees. They began to think her plan just might work. Within three years, the division was in the black with bright prospects ahead.

Requests for help are not a sign of weakness. They respond to a simple reality. Organizations today are characterized by a high degree of interdependence. Changes in one area spill over into another. Requests for help underscore these interlocking interests. Responsibility for execution remains with the new leader. But she can broaden ownership of the underlying problems by soliciting help from other quarters.

Raise the Stakes

If you have dipped into any of the standard texts on negotiation, you will be familiar with the concept of BATNA—the acronym for the best alternative to a negotiated agreement.[13] The construct forces negotiators to come to grips with a single question: What will I be forced to do if we cannot reach agreement? Its underlying principle derives from a simple observation: As the alternatives available to one party improve, the other side's bargaining position worsens. In other words, it is sometimes necessary to raise the stakes and force others to recognize that, however costly the changes may be, the alternatives are worse.

Even though an institution's survival may depend on implementing tough measures, resistance can persist. People typically focus in on the impact on their own parochial interests. Losing sight of the big picture, they assume that if they stand firm, they will prevail. In cases like these, it is essential to get people to answer the "compared to what?" question—to ask them to consider what avenues they will pursue if not the one under consideration.

Frances stepped into the COO role at a major teaching hospital right after the board rejected the extreme remedies advocated by the previous CEO and the COO. As the red ink continued to flow, friction mounted between the board, the doctors, and the administration. On an operating budget of $350 million, the hospital lost $73 million and had to dip into endowment. "The bond-rating agencies," Frances says, "were on our backs."

Political infighting took everyone's attention away from the severity of the problems. Frances and the new CEO functioned as a team. To their respective constituents they delivered a single message. Work with us or the hospital will fail. When challenged, they asked for other ideas; none were forthcoming. The CEO, a physician, directed his attention to the medical staff; Frances concentrated on the administrative side. Both brought pressure to bear on individual board members, stressing that the board needed to focus on governance and not day-to-day operations.

They raised the stakes for each constituent group by altering structural elements to make cost control more compelling. All the key players—except Frances and the CEO—would have dual reporting relationships. The medical staff was accountable to Frances as well as the CEO and key administrators to the CEO, not just to Frances. People could no longer argue that "decisions were being made behind closed doors" or that "individuals were cutting deals in private." With decision making out in the open, the leadership team made obstruction more costly. As more and more people accepted the new structure as an appropriate framework for addressing the financial crisis, life became increasingly uncomfortable for the holdouts.

The potential benefits of a change agenda do not always persuade people. Individuals remain convinced that the upside does not outweigh the personal costs to them. A new leader can force recalcitrants to reevaluate this equation by raising the stakes. Each escalation in the price attached to continued opposition clarifies the potential damage to individual careers and to the organization. As one of the women we interviewed pointed out: "People generally rise to the occasion. They want to do the right thing. If they don't, you want them to leave."

Join Forces

Peers can be drafted to lend specific expertise when your agenda dovetails with their interests or they hope to accumulate political capital to use in the future. These are the allies you target in requests for help. Other peers are ripe to tap for more active roles. Your agenda directly impacts their performance. When support comes from multiple directions, you have the makings of a winning coalition. Tamara created such a coalition by joining forces with marketing and sales to bolster a fledgling initiative.

In response to growing pressures to provide greater opportunities for women and people of color in management, Tamara was pulled out of marketing to spearhead a diversity effort. Creative programs that her team initiated, like internships for minorities, began to show results. It was then that human resources became concerned that Tamara's initiative was encroaching on their turf. They viewed recruitment as their prerogative.

Tamara was convinced that the program's benefits would extend throughout the organization and stretch well beyond the parochial concerns of human resources. She turned to her former colleagues in marketing. "Changes in our consumer profiles and the political pressures made diversity a priority for them," Tamara says. Marketing was the major function in Tamara's retail operation. The executive vice president strongly endorsed Tamara's effort and enlisted the support of another member of the executive committee. The head of sales immediately understood the boost that the effort would give to his training programs. Together, the two recommended that Tamara report directly to the executive committee.

Not only did this intercession spare members of Tamara's team the stress of having HR constantly looking over their shoulders, it increased their exposure to key players in the organization and brought the effort a visibility Tamara could not have claimed on her own. With the key support of the executive vice president, HR people reconsidered their stance. Now they wanted to be on board as well.

Alliances like these build momentum behind an agenda. They prevent blockers from gaining traction and underscore the importance of the effort to the wider organization.

As CEO, Linda Green was in a strong position to bring people on board. A major selling point, Linda believed, was the parent company's commitment to her unit.

She brought in the chairman and vice chairman to reiterate their support and then articulated the business case to members of her group. She also worked closely with human resources and the department soon became an ally. With HR's help, she was able to back up her words with policies and changes in job titles. These steps convinced her team members that she was serious about their development. When she started to hand out assignments in areas where team members did not customarily work, they had additional proof that they would no longer be isolated in their former silos.

Linda needed support in the broader community as well. She enlisted the media as an ally. At every occasion, she agreed to be interviewed and directed the talk to the traction they were gaining and the investments they were making in their current portfolio of companies. When the local business press ran stories about deals that were in the works, skeptics, both inside and outside the bank, stopped talking about when the bank was going to close its doors and started talking about its rapid recovery.

Create Opportunities to Learn

Members of any team have mixed motives. However much they want to advance the group's objectives, they also want to further their own careers. Expectations can be spelled out. But to secure buy-in, the talk must be followed up with action. To participate fully in the change agenda, team members need to be invited to take part in the process. When their contributions are appreciated, they are more likely to make them generously. When their opinions are solicited, their perspectives can add important dimensions to the group's efforts. When mistakes are analyzed, not to place blame but to avoid them in the future, everyone learns. When consequences are collectively weighed, group consensus emerges. Creating buy-in, in other words, is a campaign—one that takes advantage of opportunities as they arise and turns even mistakes into learning experiences.

Open Dialogue

Just as feedback mechanisms must be worked out with key backers, opportunities for open dialogue need to be structured for subordinates and peers as well. However pressing the day-to-day crises, there is a pragmatic reason to carve out room and time for these opportunities.

Free but disciplined exchanges bring doubts out into the open where they can be discussed and resolved, not left to fester. But open dialogue can create a forum for more than dispelling fears.

Inclusiveness draws everyone into the decision-making process. As team members are encouraged to contribute, they have the chance not only to put out their own ideas but also to build on their colleagues' suggestions as well. As active participants, team members stop viewing the changes contemplated as threats and start to see change as a process that can be managed collectively—with everyone having a contribution to make to its success.

Janet used open dialogue to move her group from a crisis mode to a place where they could work together to fix the underlying problems that precipitated the crisis.

An information technology company had looked outside its ranks to recruit Janet. Several major contracts were in serious jeopardy. It was her job to take over the department and deliver the systems to their customers. "The spirit of disaster can be a bonding agent," Janet says. But that glue is temporary. "What do you do when the crisis passes? Some fundamental changes had to be made in the way we responded to our customers."

Janet used the crisis as a springboard to discuss her agenda for change. "We needed to take apart the process and we needed to do that as a group." Janet challenged her team to come up with quality improvement programs. No element in the process was too inconsequential to attract attention in the discussions. Often it is the little things that are the problem. Gradually, by sharing ideas and critiquing them, the group came up with an early warning program. They turned the collective effort into a feedback loop by asking customers to vet the program against their notions of "platinum service." It was, Janet says, a learning experience for everyone.

The early warning experiment was so successful that Janet's group exported it company-wide. "Anyone, any time, can now go online and get a color-coded reading on any engagement: red, yellow, green, or blue. If there is an operations problem, the project automatically goes to red."

Team members are far more likely to get behind an agenda if they have some say in its implementation. As open and disciplined dialogue sharpens their understanding of the reasons driving the change, they begin to share their perspectives on how best to achieve the results desired. This active participation not only increases group cohesion, it adds value.

Leverage Mistakes

Time after time, the women returned to a common theme: To motivate and keep talented people, they had to provide opportunities for them to stretch. Work had to be structured as an experience where people could learn, one where they could constantly expand the personal resources they would need to adapt to a competitive and rapidly changing environment. Many of the women we talked to honed their group's adaptive skills by leading members through a thoughtful and collective examination of experiments that had gone awry in the past. They mined earlier mistakes for lessons about the future.

When, for example, Hope was given responsibility for launching a major new product, she anticipated problems. It was common knowledge that a competitor had a similar product in development. The sales force pressed for delivery. The product promised to fill a major gap in their offerings. Market analysis supported their optimistic forecasts. By the time Hope came on board, however, the picture had changed. The competitor had beaten them to market.

Hope negotiated with her boss and others in the marketing function to abandon the product before it went from prototype to production and costs escalated. Despite her logical and well-grounded arguments, they remained committed to production. They believed the market could support two competing products and that the introduction would round out their line. Hope's team, heavily invested in the product's development, wholeheartedly supported the decision.

Hope found herself in the unenviable position of launching a product she was convinced would fail. Whatever she did had considerable risk attached. She decided her best course was to help the group learn from its mistakes if the product did, in fact, fail. Throughout the introduction, she captured the decision-making process and tracked the losses. At critical junctures, she convened the group to review options. She always had options to propose. Rather than flaunting her knowledge—saying she'd told them so—she gave them choices so that they could make a midcourse correction without losing face. Eventually the data became so compelling that they decided to abandon the project.

People can get defensive when mistakes are put on the table. Hope took deliberate steps to prevent that from happening. Although she was on record as opposing the launch, she presented her ideas in a way that focused everyone on the realities of a rapidly changing market and what they could do in the future to adapt more quickly to altered circumstances. In high-risk environments, people stumble. To convert those missteps to learning experiences, you have to focus not on the *who* but on the *why*.

Take Chances

When researchers went looking for the habits of visionary companies, they turned up some surprising results. For example, 3M had no master plan, little structure, and no charismatic leader. Instead, the company had developed a culture where smart people were not afraid "to try a lot of stuff and keep what works."[14] Coming into a visible and demanding assignment, you have to be prepared to take calculated risks—on people and on ideas. Otherwise you remain captive to the status quo—and that usually needs to be changed.

When Christine was promoted to head marketing for a software firm, she brought a lot of management skill to the table—but not much technical expertise. "My forte is handling people, not bytes," she says. Christine believed top-line sales could experience double-digit growth, but only if the sales effort underwent radical reorganization. In the current model, the account executive controlled all the client contact.

As client problems and technology became ever more complex, that model was breaking down.

Christine put together an experimental team with senior salespeople and technical people. The sales organization was skeptical and secretly predicted the experiment would fail. Instead, the new teams worked.

> The technical people loved it. They actually got to see the client. The clients loved it because they got a better sense of the value-added in the company's products. And sales loved it, of course, because it was easier to close the deal.

Christine took a chance on an idea. Rearranging the sales teams, she thought, would force members of her team—the technical experts and sales staff—to reframe the way they looked at the sales process. She also took a chance on her people. The technical groups had never made sales calls. They saw the new teams as a vote of confidence in them personally and as a vindication of their work.

To capitalize on opportunities you sometimes have to take chances. This is not a recommendation to try any novel approach that might shake things up or give untested people blanket responsibilities. The risks must be calculated. But a small win from a bet with good odds can provide the results and the encouragement to your team that you need to get bigger things rolling. And if you fail, you need to be prepared to have a safety net ready for the people who took the risk with you. Without one, you'll get few volunteers the next time.

Walk Through the Consequences

Action may have its costs. It unsettles the status quo. But the price of inaction can be even steeper. If team members need to understand the benefits of taking action, they must also be made aware of the consequences of doing nothing—of just muddling along with things as they are. This perspective can help team members reframe the way they view your agenda. Inaction is no longer so appealing when it endangers future prospects or inhibits growth.

Diane's construction and real estate development company was at a major turning point. The firm could resist the pressure to expand and return to a manageable and comfortable scale. Or it could break with the past and adapt to the demands of growth.

Diane had been recruited by the CEO to fill a newly created position—vice president for administration. Her mission was to introduce systems that supported the firm's growth trajectory. The rest of the senior management team liked the idea of growth well enough, but they did not warm up to the idea that growth demanded thorough revisions in the way they conducted business.

Rather than paint a cosmic picture of the consequences of inaction, Diane broke down her change agenda into component parts. Focusing attention on specific areas, she walked people through the likely outcome of continuing the status quo. She started with simple items like vacation time. When the company was small, everyone could take as much vacation time as they wanted and still get paid. It was common knowledge that they would compensate by pitching in when projects heated up. That informal system had broken down. Monies allocated to vacation were out of control as a percentage of gross revenues. The numbers Diane presented were a wake-up call for her peers. They had no idea that vacation time was taking such a huge bite out of profits.

Diane then took up the consequences of inaction in areas of greater resistance. She had incorporated overhead controls into her business plan, the first ever formally articulated at the firm. Previously bids would go out on the basis of back-of-the-envelope numbers. As her fellow executives juggled more and more projects, could they realistically expect to keep track of the profit levels? Without systems in place to monitor work in progress and overhead burden, they would only be guessing at the profit at any given point in the construction process. By the time they realized a project was in trouble, it would be too late.

Unless the firm implemented proper controls and systems, any efforts to grow top-line revenues would be constrained. Her peers could opt for growth and change or they could maintain the comfortable status quo. They could not have it both ways.

New leaders trying to build support behind a change agenda can underscore the obvious benefits—the opportunities that will be created for individuals and for the organization. But they must also make one additional argument: Not taking action can do real damage. To fully appreciate the demands and possibilities of a change agenda, peers and subordinates must be aware of more than the benefits of taking action. They also have to understand the consequences of pursuing business as usual.

Linda Green did not have to emphasize the importance of making change at Clarendon Capital. If business proceeded as usual, the investment bank would go out of business. Although the scenario was crystal clear to her, she spelled it out for her team.

Linda challenged her team to take hold of their future. They could turn the operation around. Firmly convinced, she shared the reasons behind her conviction. They had made mistakes in the past. They could learn from them and from each other. Dismantling the interoffice fiefdoms, she opened channels of communication and created opportunities for her team members to grow. As Linda negotiated buy-in, she simultaneously became both encouraging coach and disciplined enforcer of rigorous standards.

"The chairman was not afraid to allow me to make the decisions on which companies we would support," Linda says. That message sent a positive signal to her team. They saw that she was willing to stand up and support their decisions. But Linda also pushed the parent company in areas that brought immediate benefits to the group. All these moves—some little, some more consequential—showed Linda's team that she cared about them as individuals. When executives departed, she moved offices around. She made sure that someone with an internal office got an office with a window.

As Linda perused the group's accomplishments, she made adjustments in the gradings so that the titles made sense. "That was terrific," she says, "because people finally had titles that matched their responsibilities and helped their interactions on the outside." She also handed out promotions where they were merited.

These moves resonated with the group. Internal space allocations she could do on her own. But she had to get approval for any promotions. Everyone in the unit knew that she had gone to bat for them when the changes in titles and the promotions started to come through.

Even though it was standard policy within the parent, the Clarendon Capital team had never had systematic evaluations. So Linda introduced a system of individual goal planning. It was her way of communicating: "We are a unit; we are moving forward; I want to show you a career path." These review sessions gave Linda the opportunity to praise and to coach.

> *Here's what you are good at; here's what you need to work on. Let's talk about how to get you better. My suggestions for focus might be something like, "You know exactly what you are doing, but your presentations don't showcase your ideas as well as they might. How might you get people more involved?"*

Linda explicitly asked for help. She was unfamiliar with the intricacies of venture capital, but to learn more of the venture world she did not seek advice from the most senior team member on the venture side. She turned to its most junior partner. "Here's what I don't know and I need to know about this. Will you help me to learn?" Linda was open about her gaps. She was equally candid about her expertise—coming up with creative yet realistic solutions.

> *Help me understand the more technical aspects, and I'll help you understand how we are going to work through this mess. People were thrilled that I admitted what I didn't know. But I was also warning them not to judge me as an idiot. You can ask for help, but you also must show where you are strong.*

One of the critical changes Linda Green made was to introduce a long-term compensation plan for her team. This effort contributed to the rapid buy-in she negotiated for her agenda. Previously the lion's share of benefits went to three people. "Are my people going to work long hours to turn the unit around only to enrich the top two or three people?" she asked. Linda designed and got approval for a plan that included everyone—even the most junior loan officer. But Linda also shifted the plan's payout. Half the benefits would vest over four years. The rest of the payout would come in year seven or eight. Linda was putting her own compensation on the line and making a substantial investment in the unit's success.

❖

Any leader taking on a visible and demanding assignment needs to make things happen. People have to see results. To be implemented effectively, a change agenda must have broad support. No matter how much backing a change agenda enjoys at the top, team members have to be brought on board. Their buy-in must be negotiated. They have a lot at risk when any new leader takes over. If expectations must be clearly communicated, so must the benefits of the contemplated changes. But talk is not enough. People need to see the words backed up with action. If they are going to be held accountable for results, they should have some say in the process of getting there. Opening a dialogue unveils concerns about the impending changes, but it can also surface some surprising and valuable suggestions. Motivation increases when people see the possibilities for personal and professional growth. A cohesive team is the best thing going for a new leader, but it takes work to get there.

GET READY TO BUILD MOMENTUM: STRATEGIZING TO CREATE BUY-IN

Successful leaders are not just lucky. They bring people on board and motivate them to get behind their agenda.

Competence does not guarantee buy-in, nor are imposed solutions likely to be accepted if they do not square with the needs of team members and peers. Buy-in depends on convincing peers and team members alike that they will be better off getting behind your agenda and worse off if they don't.

Go on a Listening Tour

To support a change agenda, team members must be convinced that their opinions will be heard—that they matter. Attentive listening—active curiosity—is a powerful signal. Listening tours enable you to get a better sense of your team members as individuals and as a group.

- What are the interests of individual team members? What frustrates them? What problems do they see with how work gets done?
- In what areas does the group function efficiently? What are the group's most pressing concerns? What legitimate reasons might

team members have to resist your agenda? Are you open to revisions based on what you hear?

- How do your external customers and internal clients view your team? What approaches respond to their needs? What can be improved?

Help Solve Problems

Change usually creates anxiety. Addressing problems early can quiet individual fears and make the group both more cohesive and more productive.

- What can you do for individuals in your group so that their assignments fit their personal objectives? If they want to be stretched, can their positions be reconfigured? If they are not performing well, what training or coaching can you offer? How will you move out the people who cannot be coached?
- Are there any immediate actions you can take to address the group's most pressing concerns? Can procedures or systems be modified to make everyone's work easier? Can you improve communication and facilitate the way the group handles differences?
- What changes can you make to enhance relationships between your group and key users or clients?
- Are you avoiding certain issues? (These may be the ones you need to confront right away.)

Forge Broad Links

Allies and partners can build momentum behind your agenda. They also increase the comfort level of your team members.

- What interests do other groups have that mesh with yours? What steps can you take to advance their agendas?
- What are the costs to other groups if they do not get behind your agenda? Have you made those costs clear to the relevant stakeholders?

Create Opportunities to Learn

An ability to adapt to changing circumstances is key today. Adaptive skills do not have a long shelf life. They require constant renewal.

- What formal and informal processes are in place for people to learn new skills?
- Have you created structured opportunities for dialogue on your agenda? On current projects? On mistakes? On where the group or the organization is going?
- Can you float an experimental idea—keeping it if it turns out well and discarding it quickly if it doesn't? Is there a safety net to protect people when experiments fail?

CHAPTER 5

MAKE A DIFFERENCE

The Big Challenge

L eadership is always a risky business.[1] The statistics are alarming for leaders taking on new roles or assuming more visible responsibility. Not only do they frequently fail to make a difference, they often do not meet their own goals or live up to the expectations set for them.[2] It is these times of pivotal change—the shift from manager to leader and movement upward in an organization—that our interviews chronicle.

The Catalyst study mentioned in the Introduction confirmed what many of the leaders we interviewed already knew.[3] Certain sectors of the economy and specific companies are more hospitable to women than others. The women we interviewed sought out organizations where they *could* contribute and where those contributions *would* be recognized. In other words, they searched for environments that were consistent with their personal styles and their own internal value systems and they negotiated to make the specific roles fit their work and personal lives.

Linda Green, featured in Chapter Four, looked for and got reassurance on the core ethics of Clarendon Capital's top management. "A principled atmosphere is very much set at the top," she says. She could undertake the turnaround confident that no one in the parent company would mislead her or pressure her to cut corners. Alice Lind, profiled in Chapter One, drilled deep to test whether the company's professed commitment to its employees was real. "Everyone says that. They all claim they value their people," she says. From personal experience, Alice had learned the cost of working in environments that paid only lip service to this commitment. She had reported to some incredibly smart people, but found much of her time spent "managing difficult bosses." Any contribution she hoped to make on this new assignment—which carried responsibility for pulling together the right team—hinged on the congruence between what the company said it valued and the practical realities driving its operations. In interview after interview, she quoted the company's mission statement without disclosing its source. "Do you recognize this organization?" she would ask. She was reassured when people did.

Leadership is difficult in any context—but almost impossible without a link between core values and the organizational culture. These are the nonnegotiables that defined Linda Green's and Alice Lind's decisions on whether to accept new positions. Each in her own way was trying to weigh whether the organization's culture was one that rigorously found and then supported good people.[4] Each was seeking out an organization where she could lead in ways consistent with her values. Donna Fernandes found that resonance at the Buffalo Zoo, as did Susan Vega at her consulting firm.

A sense of who you are—your basic values and what you want to accomplish, where you can be stretched—keeps you centered and focused when taking on tough new assignments. It provides direction as you make choices—on what battles to fight and what causes to champion. The values that attracted you to the organization also galvanize other people, so they both fortify you against the inevitable testing and make difficult decisions easier.

Frances, the teaching hospital COO mentioned in Chapter Four, had no problem with raising the stakes for everyone in the organization if they did not get behind the cost-cutting regime needed to save the institution.

> The hospital is here for kids. I am deeply involved in education and my kids' school. I make a difference there. At Children's I could complete the package. Before, my professional life had been a little disconnected from that focus.

These values frame her decisions on the job. Indeed, the women whose stories we have recounted all believed in what they were doing. Their commitment to that work and to their organizations made it possible for them to hold a vision and energize others. Donna Fernandes wanted to transform the Buffalo Zoo so that it could become a rallying symbol of community revitalization. Linda Green wanted to restore a failing organization's reputation and lay a solid foundation for future growth. Susan Vega wanted to help her partners adapt to difficult market conditions so that they—and their organization—could flourish. These women—and the many others featured in this book—were committed to making a difference.

By a high percentage, the women who made a difference in their organizations knew early on what they wanted to accomplish and negotiated the conditions to make it happen with their bosses, peers, and subordinates. They directed their initial strategic moves toward getting the particulars of the role right for them at their stage of life. They secured backing and resources at the outset but set in place the conditions so they could continue to rely on them. Actively enlisting buy-in for their change agendas, they helped shape their organizations' futures. Not only did they want to make a difference, they wanted their organizations to recognize and build on their contributions. But sometimes it was not easy for them to claim the value they had brought to their organizations in a currency that had value.

COMMON TRAPS

Even when the fit with the organization is comfortable and the objectives of a new assignment are clear, many new leaders still stumble. Confident in their skills, they rely on them without realizing that new leadership roles require them to stretch and add new competencies that have little to do with technical expertise. Or the difference they make remains invisible to others and their contributions never get linked to them. Or they can raise the bar so high for their success that they cannot see where they have made a difference, much less translate it for others. These pitfalls hinder their progress by limiting their contribution or by ensuring that it remains invisible or divorced from them personally.

- "I was brought in for my expertise to solve a problem, and that's what I am doing."

Expertise and technical skills only get you so far. Although it is imperative for new leaders to move beyond trusting in their expertise to deliver results, the step can be painful for some women, and their expertise can end up producing something of a Catch-22. Proficiency is often the key to a leadership track, yet it can quickly turn into a trap.[5] If, secure in their areas of expertise, they do not venture further, their competence becomes a limiting factor and constrains their view of what needs to be done. The head of one of the country's largest corporate foundations summed up the dilemma:

> A lot of women take a great deal of pride in their technical proficiency.
> That's understandable. But they keep focused on those skills. That's
> not enough. As you move from management to leadership positions,
> you need a broader perspective. You can't just wow people with
> what you know.

The impulse to rely on competence can be intense. It is, after all, partly responsible for the successes you have up to this point. Chelsea, faced with an unfamiliar situation, fell back on the technical expertise that had clinched her appointment as chief information officer at a midsized manufacturing company. Almost as soon as she came on board, the CEO charged her with purchasing and implementing a new integrated cost and inventory control system. Broadly conversant with the available systems, Chelsea went right to work researching applications that might meet the company's requirements. She quickly identified one that promised the greatest flexibility. The software could be tailored to meet the specific demands of the individual business units and still produce aggregated data across divisions for the CEO and other members of the executive team.

Excited, Chelsea convened a meeting of the directors of the three major business units. She put together a forceful PowerPoint presentation that illustrated the system's benefits. All three directors raised questions about the costs. Would their budgets bear the extra overhead burden? They expressed concern about the time their people would have to devote to the project. How involved did she expect their teams to be in bringing the system online? Chelsea ignored their worries. Convinced that the technical merits of the system were compelling, she saw only the benefits of implementation. The system would, she had decided, solve many of the problems the units were having tracking costs.

With their questions unanswered, the three directors remained unconvinced. Although they agreed publicly to go forward, they were really just "raising the white flag"—ostensibly surrendering but with no intention of capitulating.[6] They dragged their feet, explaining that they did not have anyone available to work on the project. What Chelsea had not sufficiently appreciated was the extent to which the directors guarded their information. They did not want strangers poring through their data and interfering with their routines. Although Chelsea had a great idea based on her technical knowledge, she was tone deaf to the problems that idea would create for the directors.

Chelsea saw progress slow to a snail's pace. The CEO began to wonder whether he would ever get the system he needed. People began to question her effectiveness. Chelsea's expertise could generate a proposal, but she would need to draw on broader skills to guarantee adoption.

- "My performance speaks for itself."

There is a huge gulf between bragging and claiming value for what you have done. Yet many women lump them together. Self-promotion seems foreign to the kind of person they want to be.[7] They may not want to take credit for what they consider a group effort. They may fear being labeled as too pushy or too self-aggrandizing. Whatever the cause, they hesitate to emphasize their achievements. They are happy to have others sing their praises, but they won't advertise them directly.[8]

One of the women we interviewed epitomizes this attitude. When she takes on a new role, she determines to "do a great job and hope that the tiara drops on her head." As a working premise, this simply does not work. Rather than moving actively to claim the contributions she makes, she assumes they will be noticed and patiently waits—hoping—for the rewards.

The reluctance to call attention to a job well done can exact a high price. The personal fallout is obvious. Without judicious prompts, key people in the organization can remain unaware of what has been accomplished. This can be particularly true when the work is invisible, in the sense that it involves actions like team building, integration, and anticipating problems.[9] When achievements go unrecognized, a new leader can find it increasingly difficult to attract talent or resources. The organizational fallout is less obvious. Unless a new leader draws attention to innovative programs or initiatives, they remain invisible. Not only are neither you nor your people credited, the organization cannot learn from your efforts.

Stephanie missed just such an opportunity by keeping quiet about the improvements she was making. She had created a new operational model in one of her company's new plants. When an older plant started having quality control problems, Stephanie was the logical person to straighten it out.

> The order flow coming from sales was more erratic than it needed to be. Production and QC kept accusing each other of fault, and sales kept on taking orders and making promises production couldn't meet. In going over the order flow, I noticed that requisitions from sales often got held up—perhaps intentionally since expense account reimbursements were especially slow. I had the controller install the program we had used at the new plant and that speeded things up.

Stephanie put through the billing changes after a discussion with the controller. She never mentioned the increased efficiency to sales.

Although she did not have to announce the changes with a self-promoting fanfare, she could have connected the rapid reimbursements directly to her intervention. She made life easier for the people in sales, but they never knew and continued to view her as unsupportive of them, favoring the operations side of things. They resented her presence and resented even more the changes they suspected she had been sent to enforce. Some of that hostility might have thawed had they realized that Stephanie was not taking sides. She was, quite successfully, going out of her way to smooth operations for everyone.

The point of promoting achievements is that they are never completely visible to others. A good deal of a new leader's work is relational—building teams, developing people—yet it is precisely this work that can be invisible and taken for granted when it is performed by women.

- "I never quite achieved what I set out to do."

It is difficult to promote your accomplishments if you do not believe in them yourself. Sometimes, we can set the bar for our own success so high that we cannot recognize when we have been successful.

Robin took on a major challenge when she agreed to run the women's initiative at her law firm. The firm invested heavily in training and yet retention of female associates was still a concern.[10] Robin designed an effective strategy that produced results. She developed and got approval for innovative policies that lessened the stress between professional and personal life that female associates confronted in a world that measured worth by billable hours. These and other efforts lowered the turnover rate among women and broadened the range of applicants attracted to the firm.

Despite this success, Robin was discouraged. Senior partners, she felt, did not appreciate the business case for diversity. They still talked about diversity in terms of percentages, implying that there was a certain threshold—a quota—that they needed to retain. They did not look beyond to the overarching benefits or to the major impediments.

They could not see that fielding a diverse engagement team brought in new business and increased the depth of the applicant pool.

Focused only on what she had not accomplished, Robin felt defeated. But that perspective is self-defeating. If you only see what you have not been able to accomplish, that is what others will see too. Robin had in fact effected the beginnings of a cultural change at her firm.

STRATEGIC MOVES

Few new leaders take on big assignments without hoping to make a difference to their organizations and to the people in them. This refrain threaded through the remarks of the women we interviewed. But their hopes went beyond the changes they had a mandate to bring about. They wanted to make their organizations better—anticipating future needs and inventing the future.

In this broader sense, making a difference is a work in progress. Contributions, once recognized, become the building blocks for other contributions. You can help the process along with three strategic moves.

- *Engage strategic needs:* With a multitude of pressing problems, it is easy to let the big picture slip from view. Yet by keeping organizational goals in focus, you can identify important opportunities and even reframe current ways of thinking about those goals.
- *Fill unmet needs:* People often struggle with problems that they do not even know they have and that do not show up in reports or budgets. What synergies can you promote, what future demands can you anticipate?
- *Make value visible:* Value is created for an organization when strategic problems are engaged or unmet needs filled. As a new leader engages strategic problems or fills unmet needs, the value of that contribution must be made clear. And that value needs to be conveyed in a language that others understand, at a time when they can appreciate it, and in a way that fits who you are.

Cathy Benko, who reluctantly agreed to head the Women's Initiative at Deloitte, exemplifies how a leader makes a difference by engaging the strategic issues her organization faces. The analysis by a group of opinion leaders at the firm showed that a women's initiative was still important. But Cathy dramatically expanded its mission. No other effort as clearly demonstrates this as the *Mass Career Customization Initiative*. Although flexible work arrangements had been on Deloitte's books since at least the early 1990s, they were not much used because people, particularly the women for whom they were designed, saw them as career killers. But the intent behind flexible arrangements was still critical for the firm: the need to help both women and men better integrate their work and personal lives. Not only was it important to women of all ages, the men of Gen Y were also demanding it.

Mass Career Customization enables people to dial up or dial down their desire to climb the ladder at different points in their careers. Everybody in the firm completed a Mass Career Customization Profile that documented their preferences. Benko dealt with a key strategic issue—turnover and the 24/7 demands of professional service work—by creating a new program that had value both within the firm and as a key recruitment tool. Her value was recognized with her promotion to vice chairman and chief talent officer of Deloitte.[11]

The women we interviewed might not always have made a difference in such a major way, but they too engaged strategic and unmet needs in ways that made their value visible. Their results build on the strategic moves of earlier chapters. In calibrating results with the resources needed, for example, they got a better sense of where their value could be added most efficiently. As they went on listening tours, they uncovered unmet needs or unrealized synergies. The cooperation they negotiated as they enlisted buy-in for their agendas was harnessed to create value. The small wins that gained resources or built team confidence increased their visibility and led to bigger, more visible contributions.

In earlier chapters our central cases have focused on how a woman in a new leadership position meets a specific challenge—whether it be mobilizing backers, garnering resources, or creating buy-in. In this final chapter we depart slightly from that format and tell the story of one woman over the course of several years. Jeanne Lewis, our subject, participated in the Michelle A. Rosmarin executive-in-residence program at the Simmons Graduate School of Management in the spring of 2003. This account draws on personal interviews, presentations, and discussions that took place during her residency. We have supplemented these sources with articles on Staples and founder Tom Stemberg published in the business press. Jeanne was also the subject of a three-part Harvard Business School case.

During that time she rotated through major functions—both staff and line—at a rapidly growing company and made a difference in each job. Although she made similar strategic moves in these assignments— say, to add value—she tailored her approach to the specific demands of the function and of the organization. What added value in merchandising would not necessarily contribute equally to marketing's productivity.

In May 1986, Staples opened its first store in Brighton, Massachusetts. A decade later, it had sold 5.3 billion paper clips and 240,500 gallons of correction fluid. The one-store operation had mushroomed to a chain with 557 stores and a market capitalization of $5.2 billion. By 2009 revenues had reached $23.1 billion.[12]

Jeanne Lewis joined Staples in 1993. She had interned at the company while getting her MBA, but turned down the job Staples offered on graduation. That was a decision, she says, she made "from the head and not the gut." She accepted a position with a financial services firm because everyone else was after it. "I figured I should want it."[13] By day two she was miserable. Before six months were out, she left to join Staples as a marketing manager in sales forecasting and field marketing.

A succession of demanding assignments followed. To prevent complacency from setting in and to keep its entrepreneurial edge, Staples had a habit of rotating people through different functional areas. By the time Jeanne joined, the tight executive team was devoting considerable effort to recruiting and developing talent to support the company's hyper growth. Candidates had to show them a can-do attitude, competitive drive, and an eagerness to learn and stretch.

Within a year Jeanne was appointed director of New England Operations, with responsibility for fifty stores and a $250 million P&L. "I was put in charge of managing people who had all 'been there, done that' for years. They'd started out as merchandise managers making $18,000 and moved up the silo. . . . I'd never run a store, never rung a register."[14]

The next year Jeanne was moved to merchandising as divisional manager for furniture and decorative supplies. Again she found herself in unfamiliar territory. In what she calls the heartbeat of a retail operation, she had never sold a product. Yet she had to create a merchandising strategy and revive the failing category.

In late 1996 Jeanne landed in marketing, her first staff assignment in a leadership role and one where she was replacing Todd Krasnow, a company icon. That job was particularly challenging, Jeanne says. It was the first time that she had been called on to lead a business unit "that was not broken." Soon thereafter, she was tapped to head up staples.com. "Staples was in a catch-up mode," she says. In eighteen months, Jeanne grew the company's e-commerce business from $30 million in sales to $500 million.

In part, this rapid rotation was a function of the company's growth. It also fit Jeanne's personality. "I've been willing to raise my hand several times . . . for what others would perceive to be career risks," she says. Tracking Jeanne's strategic moves, we can trace how she turned those risks into opportunities that created value for herself and for Staples.

Engage Strategic Needs

With the constant demands of a 24/7 world, new leaders have to be deliberate about how they spend their time. Attention naturally gravitates to problems that sound most pressing. It takes disciplined analysis to keep focused on what the strategic needs are and not get distracted by every daily crisis. Strategic needs are those that impact the organization's business goals—either this quarter or several years out.

Most new leaders are advised to "go for the big win." Pilar, the head of development at a major cancer research center, and Donna Fernandes (from Chapter Three) each went for big wins but only after thoroughly dissecting the range of options. Pilar launched the largest fundraising drive in her institute's history, but she made that effort contingent on installation of the necessary infrastructure. Donna revamped the Buffalo Zoo after warning the trustees that a huge commitment was necessary. Otherwise, they might as well give the zoo a facelift. Once Donna and Pilar committed to the big win, they had to follow through to the end.

Judging from our interviews, big wins like these are rare and harder to produce than the usual commentaries on leadership suggest. Most new leaders approach big problems gingerly, with great respect, and they attack them in incremental stages. An internal troubleshooter who specializes in turnaround situations within her company explained why:

> You can't try to do the whole thing at once. That seems just Herculean—even to you. It's downright scary to everybody else. Instead, you break the big problem down into pieces and sequence them. That way you can show people, step by step, that things can improve because they are improving. That's good for morale. It gets them engaged in defining the process—what needs to be done first. And then it creates excitement when they actually see improvement.

An incremental approach may be the only one possible—particularly if you are new to leadership roles. Wherever you sit in the leadership ranks, you must build support for your actions—and typically, that is best done in small steps. This approach has an added advantage. If something goes wrong, you have a chance to make corrections before the entire initiative goes off course.

Connect the Dots

Hannah, the financial services executive from Chapter Three, has converted the schoolbook exercise where kids connect the dots and form a picture to a finely honed leadership technique. She uses it to help top management and her own people visualize various pathways. Beginning at A, the present, what will it take to get the organization or one of its units to the desired endpoint—the strategic goal? What are the alternative paths? The costs in time, talent, and dollars associated with each? The opportunity costs?

Foregrounding strategic needs, the exercise produces a road map for making organizational goals operational. "That's what execution is all about," Hannah says, "bridging the gap between vision and tactics." Sometimes the dots are connected with suspicious precision; at those points, she says, "you need to step back and challenge the picture." Recently tasked with a major strategic initiative, Hannah discovered when she connected the dots that she had two choices—either secure more resources or extend her time line. Managers were accountable for delivering results in the present; the entire organization had quarterly earnings to meet. Long-range goals had to be delicately balanced against short-term needs. Hannah's initiative would play a significant role in shaping the organization's future, but it could only move forward if the pace was sustainable.

The dots also have a way of moving around. Outside market forces disrupt the patterns. Undetected flaws in internal processes throw the plotting off. At times like these, a new leader can make a significant contribution simply by encouraging a rigorous examination of where and how plans veered off course. Hope's unit—and her company—stumbled badly in introducing a new product into a radically changed market (Chapter Four). Rather than participate in senseless and unproductive finger-pointing, Hope engaged her people in a process of discovery. Starting with the disappointing endpoint, they tracked the dots back to figure out those critical junctures where the decision making broke down—and why. By helping everyone understand the complexities involved in any new product introduction—the many decision trees—she made it far less likely that the company would ignore alarming data or changed market conditions in the future.[15]

Keep Testing for Congruence

Strategic goals and the needs they address constantly evolve. Market conditions shift. Organizations change—people take up new assignments, new projects come online, and new technologies redefine communications with customers and with colleagues. Anyone taking on a new leadership position must constantly test whether the needs as currently defined fit with where she wants to go and with where others are ready to go. Cheryl faced this question when she considered

whether to join Andrew, a very senior partner, in his efforts to launch
an ethics practice at a major accounting firm.

> This opportunity came up before the accounting scandals made ethics a
> hot topic. I had been in audit and had to do a lot of due diligence to weigh
> Andrew's proposal. What I discovered made me aware of the role this
> kind of practice could play across all areas of the firm.

Andrew, however, had an idea of how to set up the practice.
As Cheryl tested for congruence, she uncovered a major point of
disagreement.

> He wanted to have training sessions in ethics that were no more than
> two hours long and that would cascade down—from senior partners to
> junior partners to managers. I didn't think this approach was the right
> way to go. Because of the hierarchy, people either perform for those who
> outrank them to get visibility or go silent. In either case, it gets in the way
> of communication. I thought we should mix it up a bit.

Cheryl laid out her concerns. As presently configured, the program
would not really meet the needs it was designed to address. She suggested
that they try a pilot with multiple sessions that brought together senior
and junior partners as well as managers across all lines of service. "That
pilot was universally regarded as first class," Cheryl says, "and we were
able to come out of the gate with a great program."

Testing for congruence is not a one-time thing. Changes in top
leadership, a shifting economic environment, or a merger or acquisition
can quickly change the context for the goals of a project or a division.
To keep your interests alive, you constantly need to measure the degree
of congruence so that you can adapt to changing circumstances and not
be buffeted by them.

Reframe What Is Strategic

When you're a new leader, it is tempting to take the strategic direction
as a given and align your interests with it. This approach often works,
but it has a downside. It prevents you from playing an active role in

redefining what is considered strategic. Recall Bettina, the corporate foundation head in Chapter Two. Key executives within the corporation questioned the return attached to investment in community initiatives. Good works they considered a cost of doing business. "They saw the foundation as a drain on the treasury," says Bettina. "Our initiatives were part of the corporation's civic responsibility, but didn't make much business sense."

Bettina, approached to take the lead on a pivotal community undertaking in childhood education—Success by Six—designed the foundation's participation to supply that business case. She enlisted experts to help her reframe the case. She invited Michael Porter to speak to the board. The president and the chairman were well versed in Porter's work on competitive advantage, but were not up to speed on his bottom-line approach to inner-city revitalization. He got their attention quickly and reinforced their growing perception that Bettina's foundation work could open potential markets. Bettina then brought in Rosabeth Moss Kanter to talk about creative ways to partner in the inner city. Here key players saw real possibilities of attracting a more diverse labor pool.

Rather than focus exclusively on intangible benefits to the corporation's civic image, she quantified linkages to corporate results because she knew that is what mattered to her board. These are the numbers of potential customers the initiative will reach; these are the corporate programs that will be affected. Here are the areas where business opportunities can be expanded. By demonstrating these synergies, she changed the perspective of key members of the organization. Good works could actually be good business. She reframed the way the corporation defined strategic initiatives.

Soon after arriving at Staples, Jeanne Lewis was asked to volunteer for a cross-functional team. "Usually you roll your eyes and say okay, but that opportunity really opened doors for me," she says. The experience gave her a chance to see beyond the confines of market forecasting. Not only did she meet key players across the organization, she was suddenly immersed in how the major business units—merchandising, marketing, and operations—knit together.

A simple motto, addressed to the company's customers, drove all functions: "Slashing the cost and hassle of running your office." Staples started by catering to a specific market: small-business owners who were paying 40 percent more for office supplies than large corporations. "People want to save money. They don't realize they're getting hosed," says founder Tom Stemberg.[16]

Stemberg's personality and vision permeated the company. Jeanne fit right in. She shared Stemberg's passion for detail and connecting the dots.

> *Whenever I go into a leadership role, I want to figure out what is underneath the water I'm swimming in. So I dive down into the details in order to figure out what I'm really dealing with below the surface. I always think of it as a kind of long, slow dive into the detail: control freak, driving everyone crazy, learning about their business, understanding them. . . . Then I come back to the surface, which is really where I'm most comfortable. But I only do that when . . . I know what I've got in the way of challenges and opportunities and how strong the team really is.[17]*

Jeanne's first leadership role took her to operations. Despite having no retail experience, she was put in charge of fifty underperforming stores in New England. Jeanne had little time to learn the ropes. She had to "fix it and fix it fast."[18] Due to a lack of leadership, the stores were not providing customer satisfaction. Sales suffered and the company's image suffered. Jeanne concentrated on the incongruence—sprucing up the stores' appearance and directly addressing the lackluster sales staff. Over a short twelve months she returned the stores to profitability by replacing twenty-five sales associates and implementing the company's rigorous standards.

Jeanne was then transferred to merchandising, another function with P&L responsibility. Furniture and decorative supplies, potentially a profitable category, was losing money at a time when other categories were showing profits of 20 percent or more. Jeanne reframed the way the unit looked at its product line. She encouraged the group to look at more than gross margin in negotiating and buying. What, for example, did a product actually cost when you factored in handling in the distribution centers and the shelf space it took up? This reframing resulted in changing 75 percent of the product assortment and tripled direct product profitability.

Fill Unmet Needs

Any new leadership role is dynamic, constantly evolving. A job description captures the role at one point in time. Initial plans undergo frequent revision. Problems turn out to have multiple dimensions. But a newcomer, listening attentively and digging deeper, can sometimes discover needs that people did not know existed. Opportunities for innovation may not be obvious. With attention riveted on current crises, people may not get around to potential problems that are looming. New leadership roles call for creativity and flexibility. By being on the alert for the discrepancies around you, you can pick up on these signals and invent the role as you go along—expanding it, redefining it, moving it in new directions.

Solve Problems People Don't Know They Have

People cannot address problems they do not recognize. Solutions have no purpose unless they are connected to tangible issues that people have. A new leader can step into the breach—identifying the problem and providing a solution. In the course of working through the implications of her particular change agenda, she often surprisingly discovers that the answers have broader applications.

These "unintended consequences," exported across functions, can produce a win for everyone. The process is particularly helpful to colleagues who did not even recognize that they had a problem to begin with. In Chapter Four, for example, Christine supplied comprehensive research to the sales organization in her financial services firm. Previously sales managers had been oblivious to the damage inflicted on the sales process when they worked with faulty data or incomplete information. Christine's solution bridged the opposition to her newly created unit, muting its force. Equally important from an organizational perspective, it increased the effectiveness of the sales effort.

Moreover, chances are good that your group is not the only one in the organization to experience a given problem. Janet, also highlighted in Chapter Four, wanted her group to learn from its mistakes after major contracts got into trouble. Janet's company designed and installed large information systems that were mission-critical for their customers. In debriefing sessions, they isolated points in the contract process where things began to go off track. Collectively, in internal dialogue and in talks with customers, they developed a step-by-step early warning program for delivering "platinum service" in the future. The early warning system incorporated in the "platinum" program met unanswered needs across the organization. When it was adopted company-wide, Janet and her group were seen as having made a real difference.

Promote Synergies

Unmet needs can be obscured because they fall through the cracks between functions or units. The silo effect in organizations isolates problem solving and makes it difficult to detect when problems are shared across groups. A leader who spans boundaries may be in a good position to uncover these common problems and find ways to help fashion a more systemic solution. When Bridget's entrepreneurial software company merged with an established database firm, the business press touted the potential synergies and investors rewarded a combination they thought would produce cost savings and revenue growth. In the reorganization after the merger, Bridget was promoted to vice chair of the merged entity. Traditionally the role of vice chair in both companies had been to support the chairman while the executive vice presidents headed the separate functions like sales or R&D. "As vice chair," Bridget says, "it is hard to have something that is your own."

New to the role, Bridget traveled around the country for six months, visiting every office and every plant. Instead of synergy, she saw chaos. Members of her old firm, eager to ramp up sales of the latest software release, aggressively raided the customer list of their merger partner. Salespeople at the database company, however, were convinced that long-term revenue growth depended on expanding services and were equally aggressive in approaching the same customers. "There was no strategy, people were confused, and our customers were getting annoyed, to put it mildly," Bridget says.

Bridget met with the chairman, who had been something of a mentor, and he said, "Do something about it." Bridget focused this rather vague mandate by convening a small group of thought leaders—people who had a good sense of the market and of the strengths of the two organizations. She also brought in a facilitator so that she could participate in the sessions. She set one rule: they could not leave the room until they found an integrated approach to customers—development, sales, and services—and they had to reduce that solution to one piece of paper.

The group came up with a visual model that ranked clients by IT purchasing power and then linked that purchasing power to the software and services the client actually bought or might be persuaded to buy. In a second iteration, they applied the same model to their competition's chief customers, so they could detect new opportunities. "The beauty of the model," Bridget says, "is that is easy to use."

> You can see where there is redundancy you don't need and where redundancy is necessary but must be coordinated to make a big sale across functionalities. It applies to software, database management, or services—or all of them, all together. Everybody is using it.

Before Bridget closeted the thought leaders in a room, no one had really pushed back on what it meant to merge the two companies.

A new leader can also play a major role in facilitating the transfer of successful experiments across boundaries. The "not invented here" syndrome plagues many organizations, and people can be reluctant to pick up an initiative that could add value simply because it was developed elsewhere. When synergies are built into an initiative, they have the potential to increase its impact geometrically. Not only do they improve productivity, they build organizational coherence.

Consider how Tamara in Chapter Four linked her fledgling diversity effort to specific goals in recruitment and marketing. More than experiments in political correctness, her programs could directly affect the talent the retail operation attracted and shape the image it projected in the community. The potential impact did not escape the notice of marketing or operations. Marketing saw in the programs a way to brand the chain's image and increase store traffic. Operations linked them to the perceived need to expand recruitment efforts. A diverse staff of sales associates would reflect the chain's broad customer base. Tamara's programs benefited each functional area; they also made a significant difference to the organization as a whole—bringing its operational procedures into alignment with its image and mission.

Anticipate Future Needs

Unmet needs may not be immediate. But a leader who is attuned to what is happening in the organization and is well connected can be very well positioned to hear about changes before they occur. With that information, she has choices in how to respond. Recall Roberta in Chapter Two, the senior vice president who took over the IT customer relationship function in a large financial services firm. From her corporate vantage point, Roberta saw that consolidation on the IT side of the business was likely. IT people in the various business units could lose their jobs. The consolidation might also hamper some of the business units, which depended on state-of-the-art IT to deal with the volume of transactions. Anticipating the problem, Roberta worked with the units to help retain their best people, and she helped to arrange transfers for those who needed them. In the process, she built a group of devoted allies.

It is difficult to predict what will happen in the next few years or even months. But when a leader cultivates critical relationships, she is more likely to see the changes that may be coming. Access to that information positions her to step in and respond. In the process, she both expands her purview and prepares the organization for the future.

When Tom Stemberg asked Jeanne Lewis to head up a strategic business unit, Jeanne did not think twice. Although the assignment was one anyone would want, Jeanne characterized the transition as the scariest she made.

Marketing was a staff position, not a line job. Jeanne would have a big budget but no P&L responsibility. Her previous assignments were turnarounds: revitalizing a group of underperforming stores and restoring a product category to profitability. Results—progress—could be measured daily. Marketing had no equivalent scorecard. Moreover, the department had been headed by a marketing legend; she was not walking into another turnaround situation plagued by a lack of leadership. "It's a lot easier to deal with a broken unit than enter an area that is doing just fine," she says. "I floundered until I could find a way to measure performance."

Because her predecessor, Todd Krasnow, was such a marketing star, no one suspected that Jeanne would uncover any problems. But during this period the Point Team was preoccupied with plans for a merger with Office Depot.[19] The Point Team, a tight group of top functional leaders, had been created to keep the company "on point" during its rapid growth. Distracted by the merger, its members lost some of their intense focus on sharing goals and information. Jeanne, not a member, detected hints of trouble in marketing. Internal goals were not always in line with broader corporate goals. Internal objectives were not even consistent within marketing.

In the months before Krasnow's departure, Jeanne worked closely with him to ensure a smooth transition. During this period she shuttled back and forth between her existing responsibilities in merchandising and those she would soon take on in marketing. On one detail, Jeanne was adamant. For marketing to accept her, she would have to sit on the Point Team. Otherwise the group would conclude that marketing was losing its voice. Krasnow, they believed, had been a vocal advocate there. Unless she had a seat at that table, her appointment would be interpreted as a demotion for the group. Jeanne knew she was bringing value to marketing and she wanted—and got—a clear signal sent. Before she moved into Krasnow's old office, she joined the Point Team.

Marketing included two relatively independent functions: marketing itself and an in-house advertising agency. Marketing built brand awareness over time while advertising concentrated on generating traffic in the stores. Jeanne discovered that a firewall had been established between the two. Everyone drew on the huge marketing budget, but that budget was the only thing they had in common.

> No one knew what the other people were doing. You couldn't even have that conversation. No one really knew the marketing mix, how much we spent on each piece ... either in terms of dollars or objectives.[20]

With no common objectives and no vehicles in place to talk about them, it was impossible for either marketing or advertising to benefit from the experience or expertise of the others. Store managers wanted increased traffic and worried when they saw flyers or promotional campaigns from the competition. Marketing aimed to leverage the brand and build the franchise. Some ideas, however successful in the past, had outlived their usefulness and could not be depended upon to drive strategic objectives in the future. Cross-channel communications, for example, tended to get overlooked even though they would make purchasing easier for the small-business owner.

To refocus everyone on shared objectives and to promote the very real synergies she thought possible between advertising and marketing, Jeanne instituted a series of group meetings and one-on-one sessions twice a month with her direct reports.

The group staff meetings faltered. People had gotten out of the habit of sharing information or ideas. Jeanne discovered that she ended up doing most of the talking.

She immediately changed the format. Staff meetings—stretched to three hours—would be held every other week. Jeanne circulated the agenda beforehand. She would have the floor for the first half-hour; then staff members would talk about what they were working on—what was going well and what was not. The interchange of ideas and information began to create a greater sense of cohesion among the group. But the process put a new kind of stress on individuals unaccustomed to sharing or being in the spotlight. Shared understandings helped bridge that uneasiness. If a particular group had to surrender money to another department, Jeanne observes, at least they had a basis for understanding why that decision was in the interests of the overall business.[21]

From her stints in operations and merchandising, Jeanne also realized that people on the line did not feel that marketing was always responsive to their needs. But again those needs were perceived differently. Operations wanted solutions and state-of-the-art systems that would attract customers; merchandising, on the other hand, lobbied for efforts that would increase brand awareness.

Looking to the future, Jeanne knew, marketing would have to develop a plan that would allow its efforts to drive both sales and the Staples brand. She drew operations and merchandising into the decision-making process. Whenever a staff member came up with a report that affected their areas, she would make sure that the right people got a copy and asked for their feedback.

Make Your Value Visible

Any new leader has one prime objective in a new assignment: to create value for her organization. But for those contributions to have full impact, the value must be visible. And visibility can be a problem for women on two counts. First, women hold only a small percentage of line jobs—those with P&L responsibility.[22] It is more difficult to make your value visible from staff positions, yet more than two-thirds of leadership positions held by women are in areas such as human resources or public relations. Without P&L responsibility results are difficult to measure. Even with P&L responsibility, team-building efforts can be written off as "women's work" and not recognized as the driving force behind any uptick in productivity.[23]

Making value visible galvanizes your group—it validates what you are doing together. Recognition by the wider organization can serve as a springboard for future contributions. But claiming value can create double binds for women. If they make those claims vigorously, they can be seen as self-aggrandizing or pushy, yet less vigorous efforts may be ineffective. Value can be claimed subtly, but it must be claimed. Otherwise significant contributions go unrecognized with nobody inclined to build on them. Art and nuance come in selecting how, where, and when to claim that value.

Play on a Visible Field

Whether a new assignment is a staff or a line job, you want to have its accomplishments associated with you. To claim value is to have aspects of the role seen as something that you own and make happen. Rachel, the aerospace engineer mentioned in Chapter Two, ensured visibility when she and her boss worked out their division of labor. She became the public face of the leadership group—walking the floors, talking to the engineers. When problems arose, they came to her, not to her boss. The clear definition of Rachel's role as the problem solver not only increased her visibility, it pointed to her accomplishments. It also differentiated her contribution from that of her co-leader.

This differentiation can create something of a dilemma. When you are tapped for a demanding position, you can find that you report to one of the organization's stars, even a mentor. Unless you take care to establish your own identity, your contributions can get lost in your boss's achievements. Cheryl, discussed earlier in this chapter, faced this prospect when she joined Andrew in his effort to start an ethics practice in their accounting firm.

> Andrew had this great idea. Everyone attached it to him. He had connections, built over time, throughout the firm, across all lines of business and had marshaled the resources to get the practice off the ground.

Starting out, the practice was clearly identified with Andrew. "He wanted someone to do the day-to-day work," Cheryl says. Cheryl recognized the potential risk to her and the practice if she was perceived only to be doing Andrew's legwork. Cheryl, however, had definite ideas on implementation. Specifically, she advocated longer training programs with participants from all levels of the firm. As the two talked and launched the pilot, their relationship began to change. Gradually it evolved into a partnership. The shift freed both of them. "This is yours to run with now," he told her. "You are the czarina of ethics here." Cheryl gained visibility as Andrew withdrew from active involvement and the practice gained visibility as it became a forum where thorny issues could be explored across all levels of the firm in a nonthreatening environment.

Show Value in a Currency That Has Currency

Organizations, and the people in them, have issues that matter to them. These issues can be thought of as currencies, in the sense that they have value. That value can shift based on environmental factors like the economy or because of changes in leadership. To gain visibility for your contributions, you have to show value in a value that matters to the organization.

When Ellen Zane took over as president and chief executive at Tufts-New England Medical Center in 2004, the teaching hospital was in a financial crisis.[24] She moved quickly to show she would deal with it. A well-regarded negotiator, she reopened contracts with major insurance companies to increase their reimbursements. She sold one of the buildings to improve the hospital's cash position and she changed the timing on how it paid its bills. The norm for accounts payable was below the industry average, while that for accounts receivable was above, meaning that it was paying out funds before receiving them. Her actions were literally dealing with a currency that had currency.

Linda Green, featured in Chapter Four, dealt with a different kind of currency, the perception that the bank could survive. Not only did her staff complete the SEC audit on time, she reestablished the auditors' confidence in the bank's ability to get its financial house in order. Everyone in the regulated organization knew the importance of maintaining good relations with the SEC.

Recall Bridget and the way she enlisted thought leaders in her newly merged company to help her make her case. After Bridget's captive group came up with the tools for a unified client strategy, they presented the one-page diagram to the executive committee and requested comments. The chairman, about to leave on a European sales trip, asked that members give their feedback to Bridget. Over the next two months, as she took calls from senior people, she got to know the key players in the other organization better. And she became identified with the new strategy. With its firm-wide implementation, salespeople began to work together to sell the whole package and not just their particular product, and clients were not bothered by competing pitches from the same company. Everyone knew that Bridget had made this change possible. "Her" model was used everywhere. The growth in top-line sales that people had looked for from the merged company began to show up in all its revenue categories. Not only was Bridget's value visible, it was in a currency everyone recognized immediately.

Sometimes your currency is not immediately honored and you need to help others appreciate what you bring. Gail, the hospital general counsel from Chapter Two, convinced her boss that she had the gravitas he considered essential to the role by demonstrating her analytic prowess—that was a currency he understood. But Gail went a step further and showed him that gravitas can take many forms. Initially he mistook her soft manner for weakness and assumed she would not be up to the job. With Gail's studied coaching, he came to appreciate the special value her gravitas had. Her openness and accessibility meant that people contacted her office earlier about potential legal issues. This currency, he recognized, had broad value for the hospital. Not only did it keep litigation costs down, it surfaced problems early.

Attract Good People to Work for You

Successful leaders are like magnets. They attract people who want to be on their teams. The CEO of a large consulting firm put it this way, "People have choices—there are so many opportunities in our firm today. The person we look for is the one who can attract people to his or her service line. That's the mark of a leader."

That people want to work for you is a testament to your value. Christine, the software marketing chief discussed in Chapter Four, was not an engineer, but she won over the skeptics in sales by creating a unit that had high visibility. She might not have been fully conversant with the technology, but she knew her customers and their dissatisfaction level with the current sales relationships.

> I wanted to manage my teams differently. The going model was that the account executive controlled all the client contact. I wanted to change that to give everybody more client contact. The teams loved it.... It started to get around the division: "You should try a spell on Christine's team. She's doing something different." People wanted to work with me.

By being seen as a leader who is trying new things, who has a new vision for how work can be done, you make your value visible. Others in the organization naturally gravitate to leaders they think will make them more successful and, in turn, more visible.

Wait for the Right Time

Just as contributions must be converted to a recognizable currency, they must be claimed when the time is right. Throughout our stories, we chronicle ways in which women leaders created value for their organizations. Seldom was a strategic move made in isolation. Rather, the women linked their moves in coordinated campaigns—mobilizing backers, garnering resources, and creating buy-in for their agenda.

That agenda took time to move forward, and claiming value takes equal patience. Small wins help generate excitement; allies and partners create a positive atmosphere. As one of the women pointed out, "There is a time for everything. People must be receptive." That receptivity is key both to creating value and then making it visible. Ming-Li, the CFO in a mutual funds company, attributes her success, in part, to her willingness to step into what was an extremely difficult situation. But she also learned from one of her bosses the virtue of timing when she decides to take that step.

> I remember saying to him, "Peter, I don't understand. There are things that I see that are broken. Why aren't you taking the lead in fixing them?" He looked at me and he said, "Ming-Li, there is a time for everything."

She put that advice to good use and tempered her impatience in a potentially divisive situation. Her firm was involved in a major acquisition, and the president seemed likely to tap one of his protégés to head the team.

> When I first received the material from my boss, I spent four or five hours pulling everything apart. After that I had a pretty good idea about what we should do and what process would get us there. But I held back giving my ideas and waited. As expected, the president gave the assignment to Bill. Bill's a nice guy, but he doesn't know this line of business very well.

Even though Bill did not report to Ming-Li, she offered her help. "This looks really involved. Let me know if you need any resources." Grateful, Bill admitted that he needed help and assured Ming-Li that he would call her. She let it go for a while. He struggled for several weeks, and his progress was slow. Noting the general frustration at the project's pace, Ming-Li asked to attend future meetings to help. Bill was delighted.

> So now I am playing a major role in the project. I am training them and acting as a kind of adviser. What is so interesting is that because Bill and his staff bring up my name so much in front of the president, he has begun to see me as the de facto leader of the project.

Later, the president thanked Ming-Li for her efforts. She did not let the opportunity pass: "Fine, as long as you don't forget to recognize the effort." Subsequently the president broadcast how well the process had worked. "Their learning curve just kept going." Recognizing that despite her contribution, she had to wait to create value, Ming-Li had slowly made it visible to the president and others in the financial group.

This message—and the recognition behind it—underscored an important skill set Ming-Li was patiently trying to develop among key associates in her own group. Although the results of helping and coaching did not show up immediately on her bottom line, they contributed to the collaborative culture she wanted to cultivate. She devoted considerable time to developing talent, and the organization as a whole valued that work. She claimed value for her invisible work.

In 1999 Jeanne Lewis was appointed president of staples.com. "Staples was in catch-up mode," she says. But to compete effectively—and for the online enterprise to have any credibility—Jeanne needed two things: an ability to attract dot-com talent and a way to defuse potential opposition from the bricks-and-mortar side. Jeanne outlined the dual problems to the CEO and the CFO. Tracking stock, the CFO suggested, might provide the right incentive for the dot-com contingent. Jeanne built on the idea, proposing that everyone, including the bricks-and-mortar folks, be able to participate in the IPO. The rapid deterioration in the appetite for IPOs, particularly Internet offerings, curtailed these plans, but Jeanne's objective was clear. Staples needed to move ahead before the competition did. Jeanne considered it dangerous to compartmentalize Internet strategy and bricks-and-mortar strategy. She had witnessed the long-standing competition between the stores and the catalogue operation, Staples Direct. Store managers feared they would lose control of their customers.

Jeanne set out to prove that they were not playing a zero-sum game. "Many of our customers shop across all three channels—stores, catalogue, and Web site. And, when they do, they spend on average 4.5 times as much per year as customers who shop only in the stores. Multiple channels generate enormous buying power." Unconstrained by shelf space, the online Staples could offer a broader selection of hardware and accessories with an even greater selection of software titles.

Moreover, the online site could help the stores and merchandising, whose biggest headache was old stock. "Old Post-it notes aren't much of a problem; old PCs are." On Jeanne's watch, the Internet became a channel for clearing inventory. She wanted to prove that they were "in this all together."

Right after she took over at staples.com, she gave a speech to three thousand general managers.

> I talked about the Internet and then I told them to look under their chairs. I had had chocolate boats made—half said Staples, the other half staples.com—and put one under each chair. I asked everyone to pick up their boat and see if they had the right one. There was a lot of confusion. I let it go on for a bit, then said: Stop. We are all in the same boat. It was a real Ah-ha moment. People saw how silly the worries about cannibalization were.

Although Jeanne took great care to establish synergies across the channels and functional disciplines, she also wanted to establish an identity for staples.com. Meg Whitman was on the Staples board and Jeanne enlisted her as a mentor to learn about what she did at eBay. Electing to remain in the same building that housed the bricks-and-mortar operations, she created a new environment for staples.com. Walls were painted white, instead of Staples brown. Separate offices became open cubicles. And cookies were put out to welcome everyone. The changes fit the Internet culture. Everyone she was hiring was under twenty-five. Communication became direct. Once the cubicles appeared, Jeanne's e-mail and voice mail dropped precipitously. People talked to each other, face-to-face, accelerating decision making. In fourteen months, staples.com went from $30 million in sales to $500 million and turned a profit two years ahead of schedule.

After nine years with the company, Jeanne was asked to return to the core business as third in line to run the company. Although she initially agreed, she changed her mind and resigned in December 2001 because she wasn't excited about the role she'd be taking. "For eight and a half years it didn't feel like work." Coming full circle—to where her style and interests align with the culture—she is now part of an international consultancy that both advises clients and executes critical strategic, business, and financial initiatives on their behalf.[25]

Some of the women we interviewed searched hard to find an organization where they could make a difference, one that fit their values and the difference they wanted to make. Ming-Li, the chief financial officer who claimed value patiently, took what appears, from a cursory look at her résumé, a circuitous path. She, however, sees a logical pattern.

> When I move I always have reasons for the move. I don't move for money or title. That's secondary. Each move validates a piece of you. I knew what I could do in a function—say, in accounting or finance. What else could I do? What is my potential? Where are my limits? Could I excel in something I have never done before? Try it out—that has always been my goal. I call it self-growth—recognition of a career as a work in progress.

Leadership—like a career—is inherently a work in progress. It is a process of constant adaptation and growth—experimenting, keeping what works and jettisoning what does not. Each strategic step taken leads to another just as the difference you make becomes a springboard for other contributions.

GET READY TO MAKE A DIFFERENCE: STRATEGIZING TO CREATE VISIBILITY AND CLAIM VALUE

You can make a difference—for other people, for your organization—but it is up to you to make your value visible.

In creating value in a new role it is easy to focus on what you know best and ignore the bigger challenges. In the pressing demands of any new position, it is also tempting to think only about what you have not yet accomplished or to assume that your achievements will be obvious to others without any prompting.

- Who in the organization needs to know about the results you and your group have produced? Have you made any efforts to bring those contributions to their notice? Or have you taken it for granted that the results will command attention simply on their own merits?

- What in your mind would be a great outcome? Are those results a stretch, but still within reach? Or have you set the bar so high that you sometimes think you are not accomplishing much of anything?

Engage Strategic Needs

Effective leaders keep the current business humming while simultaneously planning ahead—anticipating the turns in the roadway.

- How clear are you regarding the organization's strategy and the part your unit plays in furthering strategic objectives? How clear are others? What steps can you take to dispel any confusion that may exist?
- As you identify existing problems, do you find points where current strategic approaches come up short? Are there ways that you can help others reframe how they define those problems? Where would your input be most useful in reshaping perceptions of the organization's strategic needs?
- What existing management practices or other performance drivers may impede or stall progress? What changes can you suggest? To whom? When and how?

Fill Unmet Needs

It is hard to solve a problem that you do not realize you have. It is also hard to solve common problems when people are siloed in independent groups.

- From your vantage point, what unmet needs can you see? How might you address them?
- Which of your projects have potential relevance for other groups? How can you facilitate the sharing of information?
- What changes can you anticipate that will affect other people? How can you help them to maximize positive change? Minimize negative change?

Make Your Value Visible

The value you create will remain invisible if you do not claim it. But you have to find ways to make your value visible that suit you yet are attuned to the organization's culture. Otherwise the message won't get across.

- How easily and how often can you measure your results? How can you describe what you have done in language that has resonance?
- How does your contribution fit with what your organization values? How can you close any gaps between your contribution and what is valued? If necessary, how can you change minds about the results that are valued?
- What is your reputation as a leader? Do people want to work with you? Do people with whom you work tell others about how great it is to be on your team? Or do you have trouble attracting people to work with you? If so, why? What can you do to change those perceptions?
- Have you created a personal plan to make your value visible? Here are some steps to take:
  - Make a list of people in the organization who should know about what you have accomplished.
  - Outline points that should be emphasized.
  - Think about how to translate those contributions into a currency your audience will recognize and honor.
  - Consider how you will be most comfortable in communicating your accomplishments, the accomplishments of your group. Talk to trusted colleagues about what methods work for them.
  - Seed your visibility efforts by starting with your own networks within the organization.
  - Take timing into account. When is the moment right for each phase in your visibility campaign?
  - Develop measures to assess how well your visibility plan is working.

APPENDIX
A

A ROAD MAP
TO NEGOTIATING
THE FIVE CHALLENGES

INTRODUCTION   1

CHALLENGE 1: DRILL DEEP   19

Common Traps   21

Strategic Moves   27

◆

WHAT ORGANIZATIONS CAN LEARN FROM HOW WOMEN LEADERS NEGOTIATE THE FIVE CHALLENGES

It is clear that organizations benefit when they can make maximal use of all their talent. As discussed in the Introduction, the evidence is clear that organizations that make it possible for their women to succeed realize significant performance benefits. At the same time, the presence of unexplored second-generation gender issues, issues that are not based on overt bias and intention, creates a set of challenges for women to succeed in leadership.

This book explores how women leaders successfully negotiate five challenges critical to their success. It is written for individuals. But as we interviewed women leaders and captured their insights, we realized that organizations, too, could learn something from the women whose stories we have featured. While these observations may not apply to all women, it is clear that organizations can play a major role in supporting women they select for leadership roles, once they recognize those challenges and their consequences.

FIVE CHALLENGES TO LEADERSHIP SUCCESS

This Appendix turns the tables and looks at the five challenges from an organizational perspective: What can organizations do to complement the efforts of women (and men) as they negotiate the conditions for their success? Traps can catch the unvigilant organization just as easily as they ensnare individuals.

Challenge 1: Drill Deep—Negotiate the Intelligence for Informed Decisions

Common Traps
- "She looks as if she might be the right person, but we'll just have to see."
- "It would be good to have a woman in this role."
- "Some of the aspects of our culture may not fit her at first, but she'll adjust."

How Can an Organization Respond?
- Structure mutual intelligence-gathering processes to test for fit on both sides.

Challenge 2: Mobilize Backers—Negotiate for Critical Support

Common Traps
- "It's a sink-or-swim culture; let's see how she does."
- "People will take her seriously; after all, she's got the position."

How Can an Organization Respond?
- Put in place clear support and backing mechanisms to make the case for the appointment and counter initial doubts.

Challenge 3: Garner Resources—Negotiating Key Allocations

Common Trap
- "She can do more with less; she's done it in the past."

How Can an Organization Respond?
- Align resources with the assignment's objectives and recognize that access to resources carries symbolic value.

Challenge 4: Bring People on Board—Negotiating Buy-In

Common Trap

- "She'll be able to build a team; women are good at that."

How Can an Organization Respond?

- Communicate the rationale for change early and often.

Challenge 5: Make a Difference—The Big Challenge

Common Trap

- "If she's doing a good job, we'll know about it."

How Can an Organization Respond?

- Ensure that reward systems capture qualitative and quantitative contributions.

NOTES

Introduction: Taking Your Place at the Leadership Table

1 Maria Shriver, "A Woman's Nation Changes Everything," 2009.

2 Heather Boushey, "Women Breadwinners, Men Unemployed," 2009.

3 Catalyst, "Women CEOs of the Fortune 1000," 2009.

4 Joseph Badaracco, "We Don't Need Another Hero," 2001.

5 The "female advantage" was underscored by Sally Helgesen, *The Female Advantage,* 1990, and Judith Rosener, "Ways Women Lead," 1990. Twenty years later, it has migrated to the mainstream business press.

6 Catalyst, "The Bottom Line: Connecting Corporate Performance and Gender Diversity," 2004, and Catalyst, "The Bottom Line: Corporate Performance and Women's Representation on Boards," 2007. See also Roy Adler, "Women in Executive Suite Correlate to High Profits," 2001, and McKinsey and Company, "Women Matter," 2007.

7 NBC Universal, "The Female Factor," 2009.

8 Christian Dezso and David Gaddis Ross, " 'Girl Power,' " 2008.

9 Robert Kabacoff, "Gender and Leadership in the Corporate Boardroom," 2000. For a review of these studies, see Deborah Merrill-Sands and Deborah Kolb, "Women as Leaders," 2001.

10 Vipin Gupta, Sylvia Maxfield, Mary Shapiro, and Susan Hass, "Risky Business," 2009.

11 The White House Project, "Benchmarking Women's Leadership," 2009.

12 Geraldine Fabrikant, "The Female Factor," 2009.

13 National Association of Women Lawyers, "Report of the Fourth Annual National Survey on Retention and Promotion of Women in Law Firms," 2009.

14 Lisa Belkin, "The Opt-Out Revolution," 2003.

15 Pamela Stone, *Opting Out*, 2007.

16 Pamela Stone, *Opting Out*, 2007, and Joan Williams, *Unbending Gender*, 2000.

17 Linda Babcock and Sara Laschever, *Women Don't Ask: Negotiation and the Gender Divide*, 2003.

18 Iris Bohnet and Fiona Greig, "Gender Matters in Workplace Decisions," 2007. See also Deborah M. Kolb and Jill Kickul, "It Pays to Ask," 2006.

19 Susan Sturm, "Second Generation Employment Discrimination," 2001. See also Deborah Kolb and Kathleen McGinn, "Beyond Gender and Negotiation to Gendered Negotiations," 2009.

20 Catalyst, "Cascading Gender Biases, Compounding Effects," 2009.

21 Gail McGuire, "Gender, Race, and the Shadow Structure," 2002. See also Karen Lyness and Donna E. Thompson, "Climbing the Corporate Ladder," 2000.

22 Sylvia Ann Hewlett and Carolyn Buck Luce, "Extreme Jobs," 2006.

23 Arlie Hochschild, *The Second Shift*, 1989.

24 Shelley Correll, Stephen Benard, and In Paik, "Getting a Job," 2007.

25 Rosabeth Moss Kanter, *Men and Women of the Corporation*, 1977. See also Alice Eagly and Linda L. Carli, *Through the Labyrinth*, 2007, as well as "The Female Leadership Advantage," 2003.

26 Joan Acker, "Hierarchies, Jobs, Bodies," 1990.

27 Robin Ely and Debra Meyerson, "Unmasking Manly Men," 2008.

28 Alice Eagly and Linda L. Carli, *Through the Labyrinth*, 2007.

29 Deborah Merrill-Sands and Deborah Kolb, "Women as Leaders," 2001.

30 Cecilia Ridgeway, "Gender, Status, and Leadership," 2001.

31 Rosabeth Moss Kanter and Jane Roessner, "Deloitte and Touche: A Hole in the Pipeline," 2000.

32 Robin Ely and Deborah Rhode, "Women and Leadership," 2008.

33 Catalyst, "Women 'Take Care,' Men 'Take Charge,'" 2005. See also Alice Eagly and Linda L. Carli, "The Female Leadership Advantage," 2003.

34 Amy Cuddy and others, "Stereotype Content Model Across Cultures," 2009.

35 Frank Flynn and Cameron Anderson, "Too Tough, Too Soon," 2009.

36 Madeline Heilman, Aaron S. Wallen, Daniella Fuchs, and Melinda Tamkins, "Penalties for Success," 2004. See also Hannah Bowles, Linda Babcock, and Kathleen L. McGinn, "Social Incentives for Gender Differences in the Propensity to Initiate Negotiations," 2007.

37 Robin Ely, "The Effects of Organizational Demographics and Social Identity on Relationships Among Professional Women," 1994.

38 Dan Ciampa and Michael Watkins, *Right from the Start,* 1999.

39 Deborah Kolb and Jill Kickul, "It Pays to Ask," 2006.

40 Herminia Ibarra and Otilia Obodaru, "Women and the Vision Thing," 2009.

41 Joyce Fletcher, "The Greatly Exaggerated Demise of Heroic Leadership," 2003.

42 Alice Eagly and Linda L. Carli, *Through the Labyrinth,* 2007.

43 Joyce Fletcher, *Disappearing Acts,* 1999.

44 Joanne Martin, "The Organization of Exclusion," 1994.

45 Michelle Ryan and S. Alexander Haslam, "The Glass Cliff," 2007. See Note 1, Chapter One for more information.

46 Morten Hansen, Herminia Ibarra, and Urs Peyer, "The Best Performing CEOs in the World," 2010.

47 Kathleen McGinn and Dina Witter, "RetailMax," 2003.

48 Gail McGuire, "Gender, Race and the Shadow Structure," 2002.

49   Virginia Valian, *Why So Slow?* 1998.

50   Rhea Steinpreis, Katie A. Anders, and Dawn Ritzke, "The Impact of Gender on the Review of the Curricula Vitae of Job Applicants and Tenure Candidates," 1999.

51   Emilio Castilla, "Gender, Race and Meritocracy in Organizational Careers," 2008.

52   Claudia Goldin and Cecilia Rouse, "Orchestrating Impartiality," 2000.

53   Joan Acker, "Hierarchies, Jobs, Bodies," 1990. See also Rhona Rapoport, Lotte Bailyn, Joyce Fletcher, and Bettye Pruitt, *Beyond Work-Family Balance*, 2002, and Joan Williams, *Unbending Gender*, 2000.

54   Lotte Bailyn, *Breaking the Mold*, 2006.

55   Sylvia Ann Hewlett and Carolyn Buck Luce, "Extreme Jobs," 2006.

56   Shelley Correll, Stephen Benard, and In Paik, "Getting a Job," 2007. See also Joan Williams, *Unbending Gender*, 2000.

57   Douglas McCracken, "Winning the Talent War for Women," 2000.

58   Pamela Stone, *Opting Out*, 2007. See also Joan Williams, *Unbending Gender*, 2000, and Sylvia Ann Hewlett and Carolyn Buck Luce, "Extreme Jobs," 2006.

59   Joanne Martin, "The Organization of Exclusion," 1994. Also Judi Marshall, *Women Managers*, 1984.

60   Shelley Correll, Stephen Benard, and In Paik, "Getting a Job," 2007.

61   Mary Blair-Loy and Jerry A. Jacobs. "Globalization, Work Hours, and the Care Deficit Among Stockbrokers," 2003.

62   Iris Bohnet and Fiona Greig, "Gender Matters in Workplace Decisions," 2007.

63   Pamela Stone, *Opting Out*, 2007. See also Cathy Benko and Anne Weisberg, *Mass Career Customization*, 2007, and Rhona Rapoport, Lotte Bailyn, Joyce Fletcher, and Bettye Pruitt, *Beyond Work-Family Balance*, 2002.

64   Deborah Kolb and Jill Kickul, "It Pays to Ask," 2006.

65   Research on gender and negotiation shows that gender differences disappear when parties have good information. Knowing what to ask for makes you feel that what you are asking for is more defensible. Hannah Bowles,

Hannah Riley, Linda Babcock, and Kathleen L. McGinn, "Constraints and Triggers," 2005.

Chapter One: Drill Deep

1 Ryan and Haslam (2007) label this the "glass cliff," based on research that tracked the FTSE stock index in Great Britain. They found that when performance slumped, the percentage of women in the C-suite went up. A recent article by Hansen, Ibarra, and Peyer (2010) does not find this effect.

2 Sheila Wellington, Marcia Brumit Krofp, and Paulette Gerovich, "What's Holding Women Back?" 2003.

3 Herminia Ibarra and Jennifer Petriglieri's research (2007) on work transitions suggests that women are more likely than men to focus narrowly on performance and not consider what the demands of a new leadership role require.

4 Herminia Ibarra, "Personal Networks of Women and Minorities in Management," 1993. For obvious reasons, exclusionary networks become even greater obstacles for potential women leaders in organizations where men represent clear majorities. M. McPherson, L. Smith-Lovin, and J. M. Cook, "Birds of a Feather," 2001. This factor was one among many that caused Rosabeth Moss Kanter early on to stress the importance of "critical mass" in *Men and Women of the Corporation*. Three decades later, new information technologies have opened access to information. As a by-product, they have also weakened the effects of the "old boys' club." E. E. Klein, "The Impact of Information Technology on Leadership Opportunities for Women," 2000.

5 Stacy Blake Beard, "The Costs of Living as an Outsider Within," 1999.

6 In *Everyday Negotiation,* the authors explore the role that both advocacy and connection play in the negotiating process.

7 Malcolm Gladwell (2005) suggests that often the best decisions happen in the blink of a moment.

8 David Lax and James Sebenius, "Thinking Coalitionally," 1992.

9 Ronald A. Heifetz, *Leadership Without Easy Answers,* 1994.

Chapter Two: Mobilize Backers

1   Ronald A. Heifetz, *Leadership Without Easy Answers,* 1994.

2   Kathleen McGinn, Deborah Kolb, and Cailin Hammer, "Traversing a Career Path," 2009.

3   Ryan Grim and Glenn Thrush, *Politco.com,* 2008.

4   In *Leadership on the Line,* Martin Linsky and Ronald A. Heifetz (2002) address the perilous journey of leading through change. One of the perils is that it is impossible to exercise leadership without authority; people need to heed you.

5   Herminia Ibarra and Jennifer Petriglieri, "Impossible Selves," 2007.

6   Joseph Badaracco, "We Don't Need Another Hero," and Joyce Fletcher, "The Paradox of Post-Heroic Leadership."

7   Jeff Zeleny, "Obama Purposely Taking Time on Troop Decision," 2009.

8   Dan Ciampa and Michael Watkins, *Right from the Start,* 1999. In *The First 90 Days,* Watkins shortens the time frame—by half.

9   New leaders can clear up faulty impressions that others may entertain about them using the correcting turns we describe in *Everyday Negotiation.*

10   The interrupting turn we explained in *Everyday Negotiation* can be particularly effective in dealing with abusive behaviors.

11   Lotte Bailyn, Joyce Fletcher, and Deborah Kolb, *Unexpected Connections,* 1997. Sylvia Ann Hewlett and Carolyn Buck Luce, "Extreme Jobs," 2006. For better news, however, see Leslie A. Perlow and Jessica L. Porter, "Making Time Off Predictable—and Required," 2009.

12   Alice Eagly and Linda L. Carli, *Through the Labyrinth,* 2007. This may arise because women, especially when there are few role models, may feel that they are being watched closely. Under these circumstances, one can understand the inclination to micromanage so that mistakes aren't made.

13   Joyce Fletcher, *Disappearing Acts,* 1999, and "Castrating the Feminine Advantage," 1994.

14   Kathleen McGinn, Deborah Kolb, and Cailin Hammer, "Traversing a Career Path," 2009.

15 This notion is based in our belief, described in *Everyday Negotiation*, that people understand their environments through narratives. They make sense of what goes on around them through the iterative and interactive process of storytelling.

16 Marcella Bombardieri, "Law Dean's Goal Is a Revolution,"2003. Coincidentally, Minow succeeded Kagan as dean of Harvard Law School in 2009.

Chapter Three: Garner Resources

1 Kathleen McGinn, Deborah Kolb, and Cailin Hammer, "Cathy Benko," 2006.

2 Rosabeth Moss Kanter was quite clear that access to resources is an indicator of your power and influence in the organization (1977).

3 Jeffrey Pfeffer, *Managing with Power,* 1992.

4 Jane Dutton and Sue Ashford, "Selling Issues to Top Management," 1993.

5 Herminia Ibarra, "Building Coalitions," 1997.

6 Deborah M. Kolb and Judith Williams, *Everyday Negotiation,* 2003, p. 96ff.

7 Karl Weick, "Small Wins," 1984; Debra Meyerson, *Tempered Radicals,* 2001.

8 Donn Esmonde, "Leadership Conquers All at the Buffalo Zoo," 2003.

Chapter Four: Bring People on Board

1 Michelle Ryan and S. Alexander Haslam, "The Glass Cliff," 2007. See Chapter One, Note 1 for more information.

2 In *Leadership on the Line,* Martin Linsky and Ronald A. Heifetz (2002) identify four forms resistance can take: marginalization, diversion, attack, and seduction.

3 Rosabeth Moss Kanter, *On the Frontiers of Management,* 1997, p. 59.

4 Robin Ely, "The Effects of Organizational Demographics and Social Identity on Relationships Among Professional Women," 1994.

5 Joyce Fletcher, *Disappearing Acts,* 1999.

6 Transformational approaches to leadership draw heavily on the twin sides of the leadership calculus: both the instrumental, task-oriented (masculine) and the communal, relational (feminine) sides. The androgynous blending may well be one reason that women can find the approach so successful in receptive environments. Alice Eagly and Linda L. Carli, "The Female Leadership Advantage," 2003.

7 The appreciative moves we briefly described in the Introduction and covered in *Everyday Negotiation* in detail fit nicely here.

8 In *Everyday Negotiation*, see Chapter 5 on using appreciative moves to enlist others to work with you.

9 Glenn Kessler, "The Global Listening Tour," 2009.

10 Jean Hollands, *Same Game, Different Rules*, 2001.

11 Deborah Ancona's research with Henrik Bresman (*X Teams*, 2007) indicates that the people who lead the most successful groups are the ones who manage the boundaries best.

12 David Lax and James Sebenius, "Thinking Coalitionally," 1992. In these "winning coalitions" momentum gathers with the addition of each ally until, as the saying goes, "resistance is futile."

13 For more on BATNA, see Roger Fisher, William Ury, and Bruce Patton, *Getting to Yes*, 1992.

14 Jim Collins and Jerry Porras, *Built to Last*, 1994.

Chapter Five: Make a Difference

1 Martin Linksy and Ronald A. Heifetz, *Leadership on the Line*, 2002.

2 Dan Ciampa and Michael Watkins, *Right from the Start*, 1999.

3 Catalyst, "The Bottom Line: Connecting Corporate Performance and Gender Diversity," 2004.

4 On an anecdotal basis our commentators confirm the findings Jim Collins reports in *Good to Great*. Great companies, Collins discovered, are those that bring talented people together and enable them to make a difference—simultaneously encouraging their contributions and valuing them.

5   Herminia Ibarra and Jennifer Petriglieri (2007) show how women tend to adopt a self-protective stance by holding on to their technical expertise and not experimenting with new roles that take them out of their comfort zone.

6   Paul W. Mulvey, Priscilla M. Veiga, and John F. Elsass, "When Team Members Raise a White Flag," 1996.

7   Women are much less likely to use self-promoting tactics than men are. See Lynn Sherr's 2003 story, "Women Learn Bragging Rights," regarding her segment on ABC News 20/20 featuring Peggy Klaus, author of *Brag: The Art of Tooting Your Own Horn Without Blowing It.*

8   A taboo on bragging is one of the conversational prohibitions among women that Deborah Tannen singles out in *You Just Don't Understand* (1990). See Chapter 8, "Damned If You Do."

9   Joyce Fletcher, *Disappearing Acts,* 1999.

10 Twenty-seven percent of female associates changed jobs within the first three years and another 17 percent left during their fourth to sixth years, but the primary economic return on investment comes after year three. Estimates place the cost to a law firm to replace an associate anywhere from $200,000 to $500,000. New Jersey State Employment and Training Commission, "Legal Talent at the Crossroads," 2009, footnotes 3, 6.

11 Kathleen McGinn, Deborah Kolb, and Cailin Hammer, "Cathy Benko," 2006; see also Cathy Benko and Anne Weisberg, *Mass Career Customization,* 2007.

12 Tom Stemberg and David Whitford, "Putting a Stop to Mom and Pop," 2002, and Staples now has stores in twenty-seven countries in North and South America, Europe, Asia, and Australia.

13 Amy Bodow, "Risk and Reward," 2003.

14 Linda A. Hill and Kristin C. Doughty, "Jeanne Lewis at Staples, Inc. (A)," 2000.

15 In organizations decisions are influenced by previous decisions. The need to justify project funding decisions can skew future decision making in favor of continuation so that sunk costs can be recovered. Individuals can

also surrender to group think. See B. M. Staw, "Knee-Deep in the Big Muddy," 1976, and Irving Janis, *Victims of Group Think*, 1982.

16   Tom Stemberg and David Whitford, "Putting a Stop to Mom and Pop," 2002.

17   Linda A. Hill and Kristin C. Doughty, "Jeanne Lewis at Staples, Inc. (A)," 2000.

18   Linda A. Hill and Kristin C. Doughty, "Jeanne Lewis at Staples, Inc. (A)," 2000.

19   In July 1997, a federal judge refused to allow the merger to continue on antitrust grounds.

20   Linda A. Hill and Kristin C. Doughty, "Jeanne Lewis at Staples, Inc. (A)," 2000.

21   Linda A. Hill and Kristin C. Doughty, "Jeanne Lewis at Staples, Inc. (B)," 2000.

22   Catalyst, "Catalyst Census of Women Corporate Officers and Top Earners of the Fortune 500," 2007.

23   Joyce Fletcher, *Disappearing Acts*, 1999.

24   Cynthia Ingols and Lisa Brem, "Ellen Zane," 2009.

25   Amy Bodow, "Risk and Reward," 2003.

BIBLIOGRAPHY

Acker, Joan. "Hierarchies, Jobs, Bodies: A Theory of Gendered Organizations." *Gender & Society*, 1990, *4*(2), 139–158.

Adler, Roy. "Women in the Executive Suite Correlate to High Profits." 1999 European Project on Equal Pay, Stockholm, Sweden.

Ancona, Deborah, and Henrik Bresman. *X Teams: How to Build Teams That Lead, Innovate and Succeed.* Boston: Harvard Business Press, 2007.

Babcock, Linda, and Sara Laschever. *Women Don't Ask: Negotiation and the Gender Divide.* Princeton, N.J.: Princeton University Press, 2003.

Badaracco, Joseph. "We Don't Need Another Hero." *Harvard Business Review*, 2001, *79*(8), 120–127.

Bailyn, Lotte. *Breaking the Mold: Redesigning Work for Productive and Satisfying Lives* (2nd ed.). Ithaca, N.Y.: ILR Press, 2006.

Bailyn, Lotte, Joyce Fletcher, and Deborah Kolb. "Unexpected Connections." *Sloan Management Review*, 1997, *38*(4), 11–19.

Beard, Stacy Blake. "The Costs of Living as an Outsider Within: An Analysis of the Mentor Relationships and Career Success of Black and White Women in the Corporate Sector." *Journal of Career Development*, 1999, *26*(1), 21–26.

Belkin, Lisa. "The Opt-Out Revolution." *New York Times Magazine*, Oct. 26, 2003, pp. 42ff.

Benko, Cathy, and Anne Weisberg. *Mass Career Customization: Aligning the Workplace with Today's Nontraditional Workforce.* Boston: Harvard Business Press, 2007.

Blair-Loy, Mary, and Jerry A. Jacobs. "Globalization, Work Hours, and the Care Deficit Among Stockbrokers." *Gender & Society*, 2003, *17*(2), 230–249.

Bodow, Amy. "Risk and Reward: Jeanne B. Lewis." Network: Simmons Graduate School of Management, Summer, 2003.

Bohnet, Iris, and Fiona Greig. "Gender Matters in Workplace Decisions." *Negotiation.* Program on Negotiation, 10.4 (2007), 4–6.

Bombardieri, Marcella. "Harvard Law Dean's Goal Is a Revolution." *Boston Globe,* Sept. 21, 2003, Section B, p. 1.

Boushey, Heather. "Women Breadwinners, Men Unemployed." Washington, D.C., Center for American Progress, 2009.

Bowles, Hannah Riley, Linda Babcock, and Kathleen L. McGinn. "Social Incentives for Gender Differences in the Propensity to Initiate Negotiations: Sometimes It Does Hurt to Ask." *Organizational Behavior and Human Decision Processes*, May 2007, *103*(1), 84–103.

Bowles, Hannah Riley, Linda Babcock, and Kathleen L. McGinn. "Constraints and Triggers: Situational Mechanics of Gender in Negotiation." *Journal of Personality and Social Psychology*, 2005, *89*(6), 951–965.

Castilla, Emilio J. "Gender, Race, and Meritocracy in Organizational Careers." *American Journal of Sociology*, 2008, *113*(6), 1479–1526.

Catalyst. "Cascading Gender Biases, Compounding Effects: An Assessment of Talent Management Systems." 2009. Available online: www.catalyst.org/publication/292/Cascading-Gender-BiasespCompoundingpEffects-An-Assessment-of-Talent-Management-Systems. Access date: Mar. 3, 2010.

Catalyst. "The Bottom Line: Connecting Corporate Performance and Gender Diversity." Catalyst, 2004. Available online: www.catalyst.org/publication/82/the-bottom-line-connecting-corporate-performance-and-gender-diversity. Access date: Mar. 3, 2010.

Catalyst. "The Bottom Line: Corporate Performance and Women's Representation on Boards" Catalyst, 2007. Available online: www.catalyst.org/publication/200/the-bottom-line-corporate-performance-and-womens-representation-on-boards. Access date: Apr. 20, 2010.

Catalyst. "Women CEOs of the Fortune 1000." Catalyst, 2009. Available online: www.catalyst.org/publication/322/women-ceos-of-the-fortune-1000. Access date: Mar. 3, 2010.

Catalyst. "Catalyst Census of Women Corporate Officers and Top Earners of the Fortune 500." Catalyst, 2007. Available online: www.catalyst.org/publication/13/2007-catalyst-census-of-women-corporate-officers-and-top-earners-of-the-fortune-50. Access date: Mar. 3, 2010.

Catalyst. "Women 'Take Care,' Men 'Take Charge': Stereotyping of U.S. Business Leaders Exposed." Catalyst, 2005. Available online: www.catalyst.org/publication/94/women-take-care-men-take-charge-stereotyping-of-us-business-leaders-exposed. Access date: Mar. 3, 2010.

Ciampa, Dan, and Michael Watkins. *Right from the Start: Taking Charge in a New Leadership Role*. Boston: Harvard Business Press, 1999.

Collins, Jim. *Good to Great: Why Some Companies Make the Leap . . . and Others Don't*. New York: HarperCollins, 2001.

Collins, Jim, and Jerry Porras. *Built to Last: Successful Habits of Visionary Companies*. New York: HarperBusiness, 1994.

Correll, Shelley J., Stephen Benard, and In Paik. "Getting a Job: Is There a Motherhood Penalty?" *American Journal of Sociology*, 2007, *112*(5), 1297–1338.

Cuddy, Amy, Susan T. Fiske, Virginia S.Y. Kwan, Peter Glick, Stephanie Demoulin, Jacques Philippe Leyens, and Michael Harris Bond. "Stereotype Content Model Across Cultures: Universal Similarities and Some Differences." *British Journal of Social Psychology*, 2009, *48*(1), 1–33.

Dezso, Christian, and David Gaddis Ross. " 'Girl Power': Female Participation in Top Management and Firm Performance." Working Paper, Social Science Research Network, 2008.

Dutton, Jane, and Sue Ashford. "Selling Issues to Top Management." *Academy of Management Review*, 1993, *18*(3), 397–428.

Eagly, Alice, and Linda L. Carli. "The Female Leadership Advantage: An Evaluation of the Evidence." *Leadership Quarterly*, 2003, *14*(6), 851ff.

Eagly, Alice, and Linda L. Carli. *Through the Labyrinth: The Truth About How Women Become Leaders*. Boston: Harvard Business Press, 2007.

Ely, Robin J. "The Effects of Organizational Demographics and Social Identity on Relationships Among Professional Women." *Administrative Science Quarterly*, 1994, *39*(2), 203–238.

Ely, Robin J., and Debra Meyerson. "Unmasking Manly Men: The Organizational Reconstruction of Men's Identity." Harvard Business School Working Paper, 2008.

Ely, Robin J., and Deborah Rhode. "Women and Leadership: Defining the Challenges." Paper presented at Harvard Business School Conference on Leadership, Harvard Business School, 2008.

Esmonde, Donn. "Leadership Conquers All at the Buffalo Zoo." *Buffalo News,* Aug. 1, 2003.

Fabrikant, Geraldine. "The Female Factor: Fewer Women Betting on Wall Street Careers." *New York Times,* Jan. 30, 2010.

Fisher, Roger, William Ury, and Bruce Patton. *Getting to Yes: Negotiating Agreement Without Giving In* (2nd ed.). Boston: Houghton Mifflin, 1992.

Fletcher, Joyce. "Castrating the Feminine Advantage: Feminist Standpoint Research and Management Science." *Journal of Management Inquiry,* 1994, *3*(1), 74–82.

Fletcher, Joyce. *Disappearing Acts: Gender, Power, and Relational Practice at Work.* Cambridge, Mass.: MIT Press, 1999.

Fletcher, Joyce. "The Greatly Exaggerated Demise of Heroic Leadership: Power and the Myth of the Female Advantage." In Robin J. Ely, Erica G. Foldy, Maureen Scully (eds.), *Reader in Gender, Work and Organization.* Oxford, England: Blackwell, 2003.

Flynn, Frank, and Cameron Anderson. "Too Tough, Too Soon: Familiarity and the Backlash Effect." (Under review at *Organizational Behavior and Human Decision Processes*), 2009.

Gladwell, Malcolm. *Blink: The Power of Thinking Without Thinking.* New York: Back Bay Books, 2005.

Goldin, Claudia, and Cecilia Rouse. "Orchestrating Impartiality: The Effect of Blind Auditions on Female Musicians." *American Economic Review,* 2000, *90*(4), 715–741.

Grim, Ryan, and Glenn Thrush. "Honeymoon: Left Cuts Obama Slack." Politco.com, Nov. 21, 2008. Available online: www.politico.com/news/stories/1108/15845.html. Access date: Apr. 20, 2010.

Gupta, Vipin, Sylvia Maxfield, Mary Shapiro, and Susan Hass. "Risky Business: Busting the Myth That Women Are Risk Averse." Simmons School of Management, *CGO Insight,* Apr. 2009.

Hansen, Morten, Herminia Ibarra, and Urs Peyer. "The Best Performing CEOs in the World." *Harvard Business Review,* Jan. 2010.

Heifetz, Ronald A. *Leadership Without Easy Answers.* Cambridge, Mass.: Harvard University Press, 1994.

Heilman, Madeline, Aaron S. Wallen, Daniella Fuchs, and Melinda Tamkins. "Penalties for Success: Reactions to Women Who Succeed at Male Gender-Typed Tasks." *Journal of Applied Psychology,* 2004, *8*(3), 416–427.

Helgesen, Sally. *The Female Advantage: Women's Ways of Leadership.* New York: Doubleday, 1990.

Hewlett, Sylvia Ann, and Carolyn Buck Luce. "Extreme Jobs: The Dangerous Allure of the 70-Hour Workweek." *Harvard Business Review,* Dec. 2006.

Hill, Linda A., and Kristin C. Doughty. "Jeanne Lewis at Staples, Inc. (A)." Harvard Business School Case, 9–400–065. Rev. July 24, 2000.

Hill, Linda A., and Kristin C. Doughty. "Jeanne Lewis at Staples, Inc. (B)." Harvard Business School Case, 4–499–042. Rev. June 27, 2000.

Hill, Linda A., and Kristin C. Doughty. "Jeanne Lewis at Staples, Inc. (C)." Harvard Business School Case, 9–400–054. Rev. June 27, 2000.

Hochschild, Arlie. *The Second Shift.* New York: Penguin Books, 1989.

Hollands, Jean. *Same Game, Different Rules: How to Get Ahead Without Being a Bully Broad, Ice Queen, or "Ms. Understood."* New York: McGraw-Hill, 2001.

Hoovers.com. Staples, Inc. Available online: www.hoovers.com/company/ Staples_Inc/rcksif-1.html. Access date: Apr. 23, 2010.

Ibarra, Herminia. "Personal Networks of Women and Minorities in Management: A Conceptual Framework." *Academy of Management Review,* 1993, *18*(1), 56–67.

Ibarra, Herminia. "Building Coalitions." Harvard Business School Teaching Note, 9–497–055. Apr. 1997.

Ibarra, Herminia, and Otilia Obodaru. "Women and the Vision Thing." *Harvard Business Review,* Jan. 2009.

Ibarra, Herminia, and Jennifer Petriglieri. "Impossible Selves: Image Strategies and Identity Threat in Professional Women's Career Transitions." INSEAD Faculty and Research Working Paper, 2007.

Ingols, Cynthia, and Lisa Brem. "Ellen Zane: Leading Change at Tufts/New England Medical Center." In Linda Swayne, W. Jack Duncan, and Peter Ginter (eds.), *Strategic Management of Health Care Organizations*. Hoboken, N.J.: Wiley, 2009.

Janis, Irving. *Victims of Group Think* (2nd ed.). Boston: Houghton Mifflin, 1982.

Kabacoff, Robert. *Gender and Leadership in the Corporate Boardroom*. Portland, Maine: Management Research Group, 2000.

Kanter, Rosabeth Moss, and Jane Roessner. "Deloitte and Touche: A Hole in the Pipeline," Harvard Business School Case, 9–300–012, 1999.

Kanter, Rosabeth Moss. *Men and Women of the Corporation*. New York: Basic Books, 1977.

Kanter, Rosabeth Moss. *On the Frontiers of Management*. Boston: Harvard Business Press, 1997.

Kessler, Glenn. "The Global Listening Tour." *Washington Post,* Feb. 20, 2009. Available online: www.washingtonpost.com/wp-dyn/content/article/2009/02/19/AR2009021903471.html?sid=ST2009021903526. Access date: Mar. 3, 2010.

Klein, E. E. "The Impact of Information Technology on Leadership Opportunities for Women: The Leveling of the Playing Field." *Journal of Leadership Studies*, 2000, 7(1), 88–98.

Kolb, Deborah M., and Jill Kickul. "It Pays to Ask: Negotiating Conditions for Leadership Success." Center for Gender in Organizations. Simmons School of Management: CGO Insights, #23, 2006. Unpaginated.

Kolb, Deborah M., and Kathleen McGinn. "Beyond Gender and Negotiation to Gendered Negotiations." *Negotiation and Conflict Management Research*, 2009, 2(1), 1–16.

Kolb, Deborah M., and Judith Williams. *The Shadow Negotiation: How Women Can Master the Hidden Agendas That Determine Bargaining Success*. New York: Simon & Schuster, 2000.

Kolb, Deborah M., and Judith Williams. *Everyday Negotiation*. San Francisco: Jossey-Bass, 2003.

Kram, Kathy E., and Marion McCollom Hampton. "When Women Lead: The Visibility-Vulnerability Spiral." In Robin J. Ely, Erica G. Foldy, and Maureen Scully (eds.), *Reader in Gender, Work and Organization.* Oxford, England: Blackwell, 2003.

Lax, David, and James K. Sebenius. "Thinking Coalitionally." In Peyton Young (ed.), *Negotiation Analysis.* Ann Arbor: University of Michigan Press, 1992.

Linsky, Martin, and Ronald A. Heifetz. *Leadership on the Line: Staying Alive Through the Dangers of Leading.* Boston: Harvard Business Press, 2002.

Lyness, Karen, and Donna E. Thompson. "Climbing the Corporate Ladder: Do Female and Male Executives Follow the Same Rules?" *Academy of Management Journal*, 2000, *85*(1), 86–101.

Marshall, Judi. *Women Managers: Travelers in a Male World.* Chichester, U.K.: Wiley, 1984.

Martin, Joanne. "The Organization of Exclusion: Institutionalization of Sex Inequality, Gendered Faculty Jobs and Gendered Knowledge in Organizational Theory and Research." *Organization*, 1994, *1*(2), 401–431.

McCracken, Douglas. "Winning the Talent War for Women: Sometimes It Takes a Revolution." *Harvard Business Review*, Nov.-Dec. 2000, *78*(6), 159–165.

McGinn, Kathleen, and Dina Witter. "RetailMax." Harvard Business School Case, 904025–6, 2003.

McGinn, Kathleen, Deborah Kolb, and Cailin Hammer. "Cathy Benko: WINing at Deloitte." (A&B), Harvard Business School Case, 907026–7, 2006.

McGinn, Kathleen, Deborah Kolb, and Cailin Hammer. "Traversing a Career Path: Pat Fili-Krushel." (A&B), Harvard Business School Case, 909010–11, 2009.

McGuire, Gail. "Gender, Race, and the Shadow Structure: A Study of Informal Networks and Inequality in a Work Organization." *Gender & Society*, 2002, *16*(3), 303–322.

McKinsey and Company. "Women Matter: Gender Diversity a Corporate Performance Driver." Paris, France: McKinsey and Company, 2007.

McPherson, M., L. Smith-Lovin, and J. M Cook. "Birds of a Feather: Homophily in Social Networks." *Annual Review of Sociology*, 2001, *27*, 415–444.

Merrill-Sands, Deborah, and Deborah Kolb. "Women as Leaders: The Paradox of Success." Center for Gender in Organizations, Simmons School of Management: CGO Insights, #9, Apr. 2001. Unpaginated.

Meyerson, Debra. *Tempered Radicals: How People Use Difference to Inspire Change at Work.* Boston: Harvard Business Press, 2001.

Mulvey, Paul W., Priscilla M. Veiga, and John F. Elsass. "When Team Members Raise a White Flag." *Academy of Management Executive*, 1996, *10*(1), 49–61.

National Association of Women Lawyers. "Report of the Fourth Annual National Survey on Retention and Promotion of Women in Law Firms." Chicago: National Association of Women Lawyers, 2009.

NBC Universal. "The Female Factor: Women at NBCU Purchase Power and Influencer Study." Aug. 28–30, 2009, and Sept. 11–13, 2009. Available online: http://womenatnbcunewsletter.com/ADVISORY_CONCLUSIONS_BOOK_E_12.31-1.pdf. Access date: Apr. 20, 2010.

New Jersey State Employment and Training Commission. "Legal Talent at the Crossroads: Why New Jersey Women Lawyers Leave Their Law Firms, and Why They Choose to Stay." New Jersey: New Jersey State Employment and Training Commission, Apr. 2009, p. 55. Available online: www.njsetc.net/council_gender/GPC_CWW_LAW_REPORT.pdf. Access date: Dec. 31, 2009.

Perlow, Leslie A., and Jessica L. Porter. "Making Time Off Predictable—and Required." *Harvard Business Review,* Oct. 2009.

Pfeffer, Jeffrey. *Managing with Power: Politics and Influence in Organizations.* Boston: Harvard Business Press, 1992.

Rapoport, Rhona, Lotte Bailyn, Joyce Fletcher, and Bettye Pruitt. *Beyond Work-Family Balance: Advancing Gender Equity and Workplace Performance.* San Francisco: Jossey-Bass, 2002.

Ridgeway, Cecilia. L. "Gender, Status, and Leadership." *Journal of Social Issues,* 2001, *57*(4), 637–655.

Rosener, Judith. "Ways Women Lead." *Harvard Business Review,* Nov.-Dec. 1990, pp. 119–125.

Ryan, Michelle, and S. Alexander Haslam. "The Glass Cliff: Exploring the Dynamics Surrounding the Appointment of Women to Precarious Leadership Positions." *Academy of Management Review,* 2007, *32*(2), 549–572.

Sherr, Lynn. "Women Learn Bragging Rights." ABC News Online, July 22, 2003. Available at: http://abcnews.go.com/2020/story?id=123678& page=4. Access date: Mar. 3, 2010.

Simmons, W. W. "When It Comes to Choosing a Boss, Americans Still Prefer Men." *USA Today*, Jan. 11, 2001. Available online: www.gallup.com/poll/2128/when-comes-choosing-boss-americans-still-prefer-men.aspx. Access date: Apr. 20, 2010.

Shriver, Maria. "A Woman's Nation Changes Everything." The Shriver Report, 2009. Available online: www.awomansnation.com. Access date: Mar. 3, 2010.

Staw, B. M. "Knee-Deep in the Big Muddy: A Study of Escalating Commitment to a Chosen Course of Action." *Organizational Behavior and Human Performance*, 1976, *16*, 27–44.

Steinpreis, Rhea, Katie A. Anders, and Dawn Ritzke. "The Impact of Gender on the Review of the Curricula Vitae of Job Applicants and Tenure Candidates: A National Empirical Study." *Sexroles*, 1999, *41*(7/8), 509–528.

Stemberg, Tom, and David Whitford. "Putting a Stop to Mom and Pop." FORTUNE Small Business, 2002. Available online: http://money.cnn.com/magazines/fsb/fsb_archive/2002/10/01/330576/index.htm. Access date: Apr. 20, 2010.

Stone, Pamela. *Opting Out: Why Women Really Quit Careers and Head Home.* Berkeley: University of California Press, 2007.

Sturm, Susan. "Second Generation Employment Discrimination: A Structural Approach." *Columbia Law Review*, 2001, *101*(3), 459–568.

Tannen, Deborah. *You Just Don't Understand: Women and Men in Conversation.* New York: Ballantine, 1990.

Tyson, Laura D'Andrea. "Glass Ceiling: What Holds Women Back." *Business Week*, Oct. 27, 2003, p. 36.

Valian, Virginia. *Why So Slow? The Advancement of Women.* Cambridge, Mass.: MIT Press, 1998.

Watkins, Michael. *The First 90 Days: Critical Success Strategies for New Leaders at All Levels.* Boston: Harvard Business Press, 2003.

Weick, Karl. "Small Wins: A Pragmatic Primer for Realistic Radicals." *American Psychologist*, 1984, *39*(1), 40–49.

Wellington, Sheila, Marcia Brumit Krofp, and Paulette Gerovich. "What's Holding Women Back?" *Harvard Business Review*, 2003, *81*(6), 18–20.

The White House Project. "Benchmarking Women's Leadership." 2009. Available online: http://thewhitehouseproject.org/documents/Report.pdf. Access date: Mar. 3, 2010.

Williams, Joan. *Unbending Gender: Why Family and Work Conflict and What to Do About It*. London: Oxford University Press, 2000.

Zeleny, Jeff. "Obama Purposely Taking Time on Troop Decision." *New York Times,* Nov. 13, 2009. Available online: www.nytimes.com/2009/11/13/us/politics/13zeleny.html. Access date: Mar. 3, 2010.

ACKNOWLEDGMENTS

When *Her Place at the Table* was published in 2004, we wrote that thanks were inadequate to the many women leaders who shared their stories with us. That is still the case. Their candor allowed us the opportunity to understand the challenges they faced and to document their creativity in finding solutions, and they continue to inspire us and our audiences as we tell their stories all over the globe in keynote talks and workshops.

Former students in the MBA and Executive programs at the Simmons School of Management took up our requests for leadership stories with alacrity. Many of these women belong to the cohort that has witnessed the increased presence of women among the leadership ranks of today's corporations and organizations. Their experiences offered a special perspective on the extent to which issues of gender have mutated into an array of second-generation effects. Members of The Boston Club, an organization of women leaders in Boston, were unfailingly helpful and willing to give up precious hours to be interviewed. Sara Horowitz enriched our understanding with stories of Argentinean women leaders. And our clients afforded us the opportunity to witness leaders making a difference firsthand.

Our ideas on gender and leadership have been influenced immeasurably by the work on second-generation gender issues of our colleagues at the Center for Gender in Organizations at the Simmons School of Management—Stacy Blake Beard, Robin Ely, Joyce Fletcher, Evangelina Holvino, Deborah Merrill-Sands, Debra Meyerson, Karen Proudford, and Susan Sturm. Others of our colleagues—Lotte Bailyn, Jean Bartunek, Hannah Riley Bowles, Karen Golden-Biddle, Herminia Ibarra, Kathy Kram, Kathleen McGinn, Debra Noumair, and Linda Putnam—have been intellectual inspirations and caring supporters in this work. Liz O'Donnell worked with us to improve the new portions of the book.

It was Kathe Sweeney, our editor at Jossey-Bass, who was convinced that this book merited the wider audience of an updated paperback edition.

The unsung heroes and heroines of an enterprise like this are our families, who helped us in countless ways. Our children—Samuel, Elizabeth, Megan, Tamsen, Kate, and Jack—inspire us every day to try to make a difference and are ever ready to test the resonance of ideas. We appreciate the enthusiasm with which Karin, Greg, Bryan, and Augie have entered the fray. Love and thanks go to Jonathan Kolb and Stuart Frohlinger for always being there.

Deborah M. Kolb
Judith Williams
Carol Frohlinger

ABOUT THE AUTHORS

In 2000, Deborah Kolb and Judith Williams wrote *The Shadow Negotiation: How Women Can Master the Hidden Agendas That Determine Bargaining Success* (Simon & Schuster). Based on interviews with women, the book showed how successful negotiators both advocate for themselves and connect with others in the deals they make. The book was named one of the Ten Best Books of the year by *Harvard Business Review* and won the Best Book Award from the International Association of Conflict Management. In 2003 Jossey-Bass published a revised and expanded paperback edition of *The Shadow Negotiation* titled *Everyday Negotiation: Navigating the Hidden Agendas in Bargaining*.

Deborah M. Kolb is the Deloitte Ellen Gabriel Professor for Women and Leadership at the Simmons School of Management and a Distinguished Senior Research Fellow at the Center for Gender in Organizations there. From 1991 through 1994, she was executive director of the Program on Negotiation at Harvard Law School. She is currently a senior fellow at the program, where she co-directs the Negotiations in the Workplace Project.

Kolb is author of *The Mediators* (MIT Press, 1983), an in-depth study of labor mediation, and coeditor of *Hidden Conflict in Organizations:*

Uncovering Behind-the-Scenes Disputes (Sage, 1992), a collection of field studies about how conflicts are handled in a variety of business and nonprofit organizations. She has published a study of the practice of successful mediators, *Making Talk Work: Profiles of Mediators* (Jossey-Bass, 1994). She is also editor of *Negotiation Eclectics: Essays in Memory of Jeffrey Z. Rubin* (Program on Negotiation, 1999). She has authored more than one hundred articles on the subjects of gender, negotiation, conflict in organizations, and mediation, and is on the editorial boards of the *Negotiation Journal,* the *Journal of Conflict Resolution,* the *Harvard Negotiation Newsletter,* and the *Journal of Negotiation and Conflict Management Research.* Kolb is regularly interviewed by mainstream media about her work on gender, negotiation, and leadership.

Kolb received her Ph.D. from MIT's Sloan School of Management, where her dissertation won the Zannetos Prize for outstanding doctoral scholarship. She has a B.A. from Vassar College and an M.B.A. from the University of Colorado.

Judith Williams spent her early career in publishing and investment banking. In 1992 Williams secured seed money funding from a private foundation to establish a nonprofit corporation engaged in researching and publishing on gender issues and women's leadership. Since 2006 she has been based in southeast Asia, where she has collaborated with women's organizations and NGOs in Bangladesh and India to increase the decision-making power and strengthen the leadership of women there. Williams earned a B.A. at Bryn Mawr College and a Ph.D. from Harvard University, as well as an M.B.A. from the Simmons Graduate School of Management with highest honors.

Carol Frohlinger works with major companies to translate business strategy into behaviors people use in the workplace. She speaks internationally, consults on management practices, and designs training interventions on topics including negotiation, leadership, team building, sales, and sales management.

Frohlinger is a former sales executive, banker, and practicing attorney. Her advice has been featured by NPR, *Martha Stewart Living Radio, CBS MoneyWatch, Newsday, Cosmopolitan Magazine,* and the *New York Times,* among other mainstream media. Frohlinger also contributes articles to professional and association journals including *WomenLegal* and ALM's *Marketing the Law Firm.*

Frohlinger's latest book, coauthored with Dr. Lois Frankel, is *Nice Girls Don't Win at Life: 99 Ways to Get the Respect You Deserve, the Success You've Earned and the Things You Want.* It goes to press in 2011.

She holds a B.A. from the College of Mount Saint Vincent and a J.D. from Fordham University School of Law. Frohlinger lives in New York City with her husband and is the proud parent of a daughter and son.

In 2005, Deborah Kolb and Carol Frohlinger founded Negotiating Women, Inc. This company offers keynote talks, corporate training, and seminars on negotiation and leadership specifically designed for women. Its Web site—www.negotiatingwomen.com—is the first of its kind to make negotiation courses for women available online.

INDEX